ANALOG COOKBOOK

A film journal dedicated to analog filmmaking

Founder/Editor-in-Chief: Kate E. Hinshaw
Analog Cookbook Logo: Sarah Lawrence Design Emporium

Published by Analog Cookbook © 2019

Submissions and Questions: hello@analogcookbook.com

Special Thanks
Jeanne Liotta, Sarah Lawrence, Andi Avery, Spencer Vaughan, Sally Cinnamon, CU-Boulder: Department of Cinema Studies & Moving Image Arts.

Letter from the editor

I started Analog Cookbook to share knowledge of analog media and connect/celebrate analog filmmakers.

When I first began working with film, we weren't in the film resurgence renaissance that we're in now. In 2012, I bought a super 8mm camera and projector off eBay. I lived in Atlanta and there was nowhere in town at the time to buy or develop film. Ektachrome had been discontinued and film labs were shutting down. So I went online and dug through message boards. I learned to develop film at home in my bathroom and hung super 8mm on coat racks to dry. I read Helen Hill's *Recipes for Disaster*. Having seen *Removed* by Naomi Uman, I experimented with nail polish and bleach. I still remember the first time I ran hand-painted super 8mm through my projector–it was magical and from that moment on, I was hooked.

Now, seven years later, here we are with film labs back up and running and ektachrome being distributed by Kodak again. I have to say, it's pretty damn validating.

My hope is that this publication reaches the nutty film weirdo developing film in their bathroom, the filmmaker making those DIY-kinda films that others think are a hot mess, or the filmmaker who wields their camera at punk shows like a knife to fend off the mouth breathers who dare ask if your camera is real or not.

As filmmaker Paul DeSilva puts it, "out with the bro and in with the weirdo." In short: I hope this publication makes you feel a little less alone in the world.

From one film weirdo to another,

Kate E.

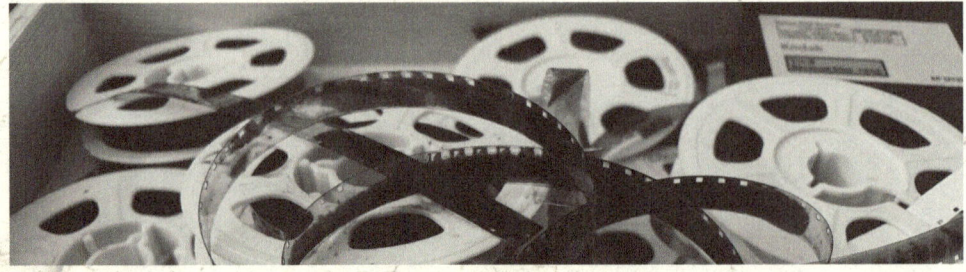

Table of Contents

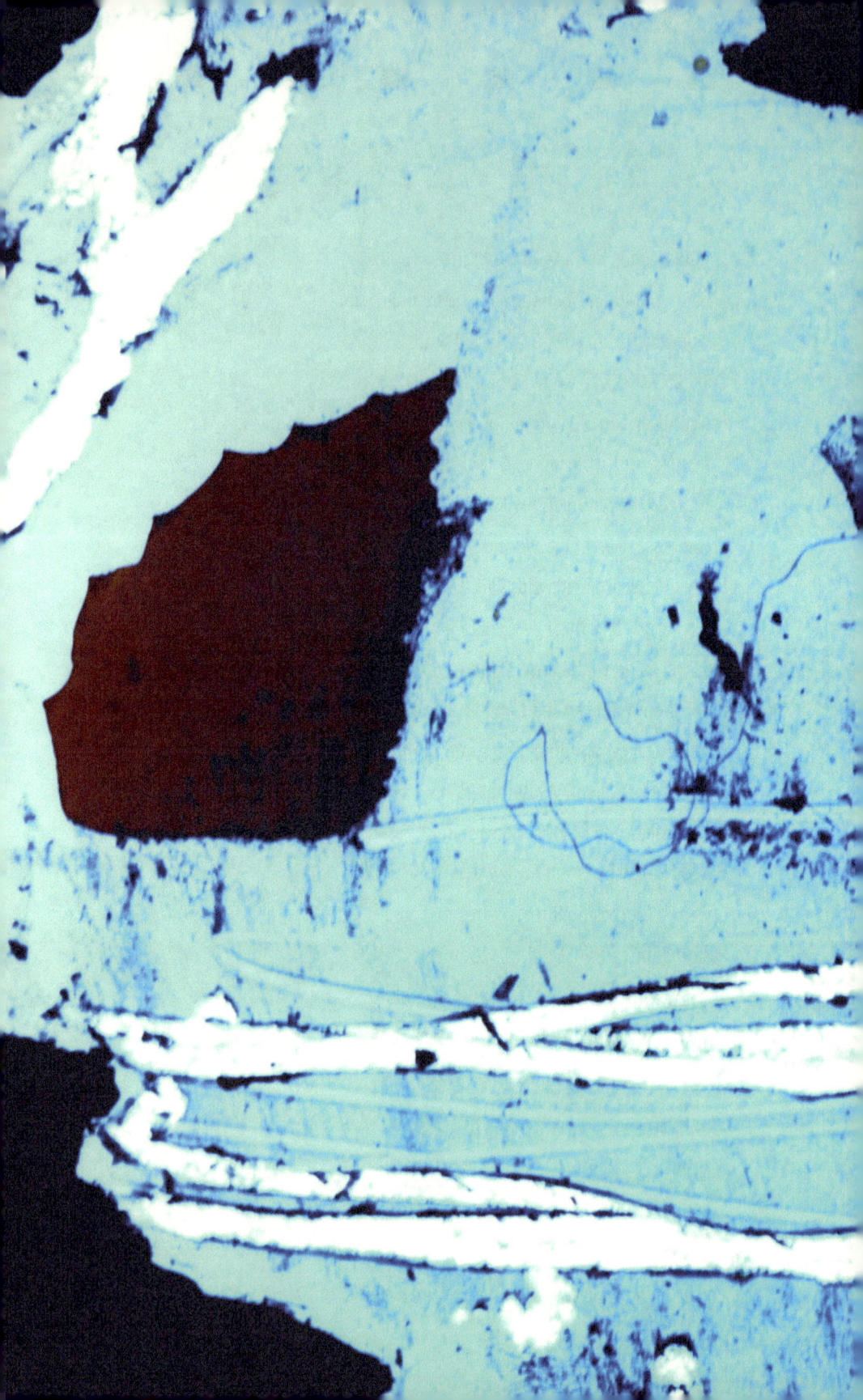

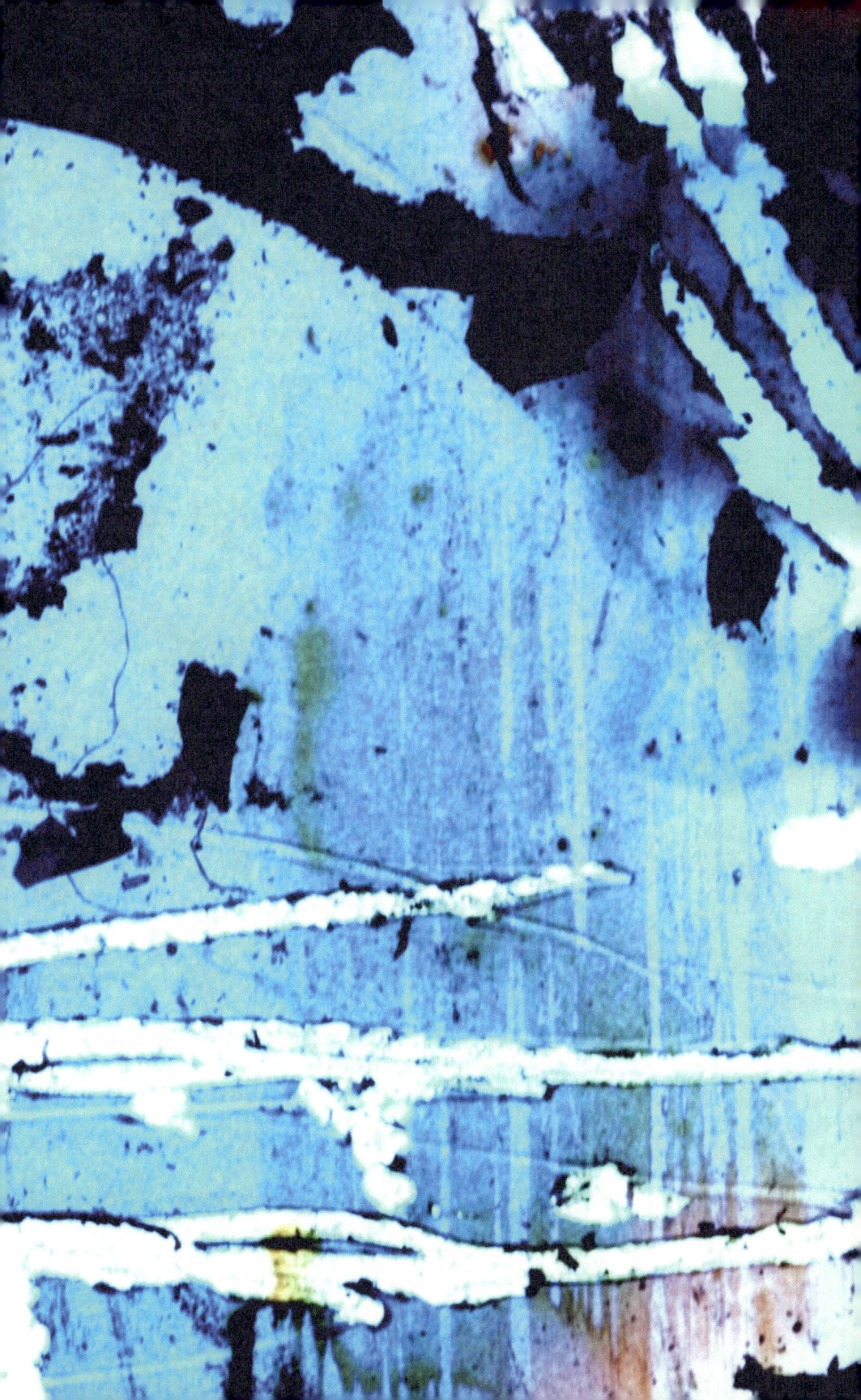

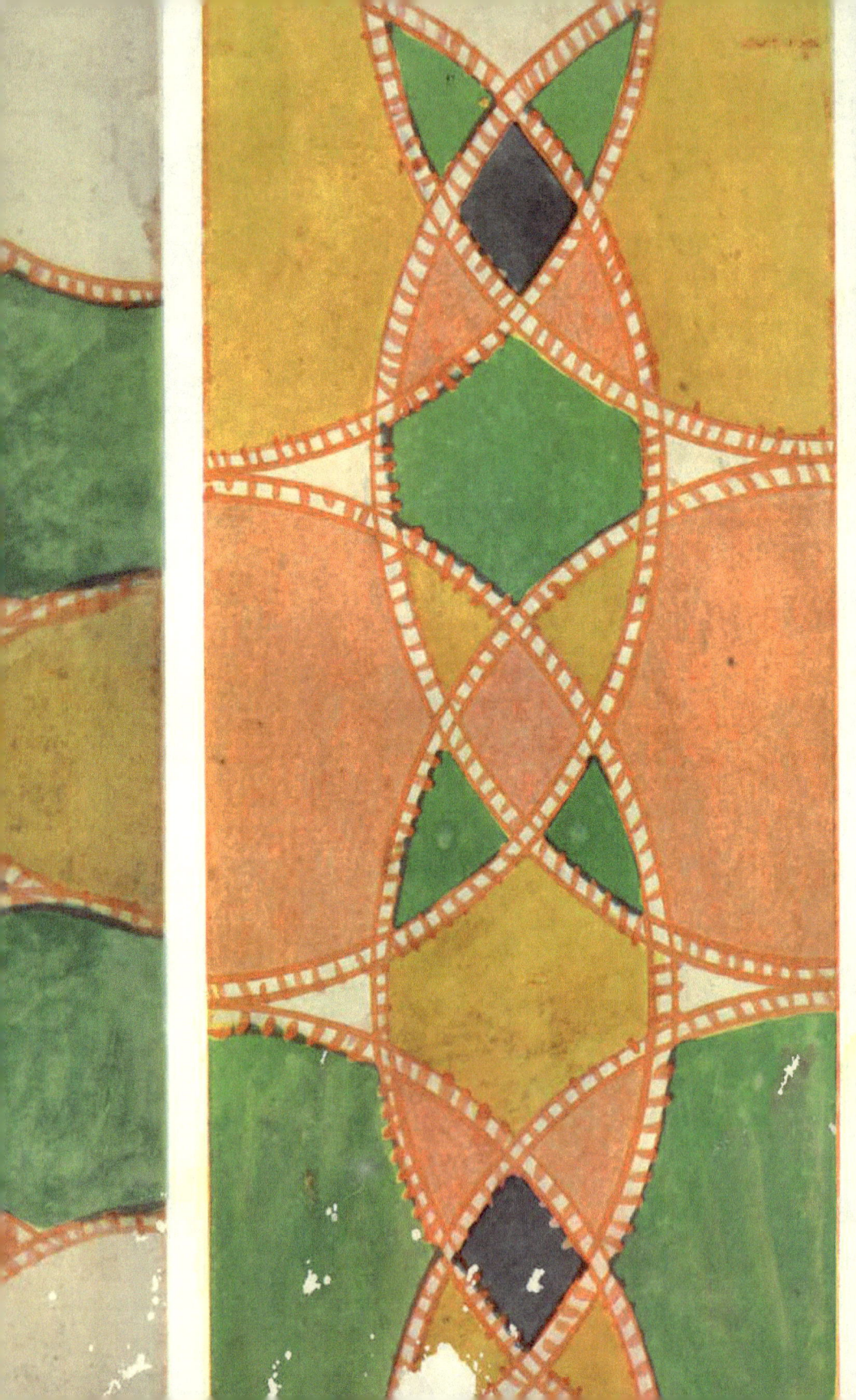

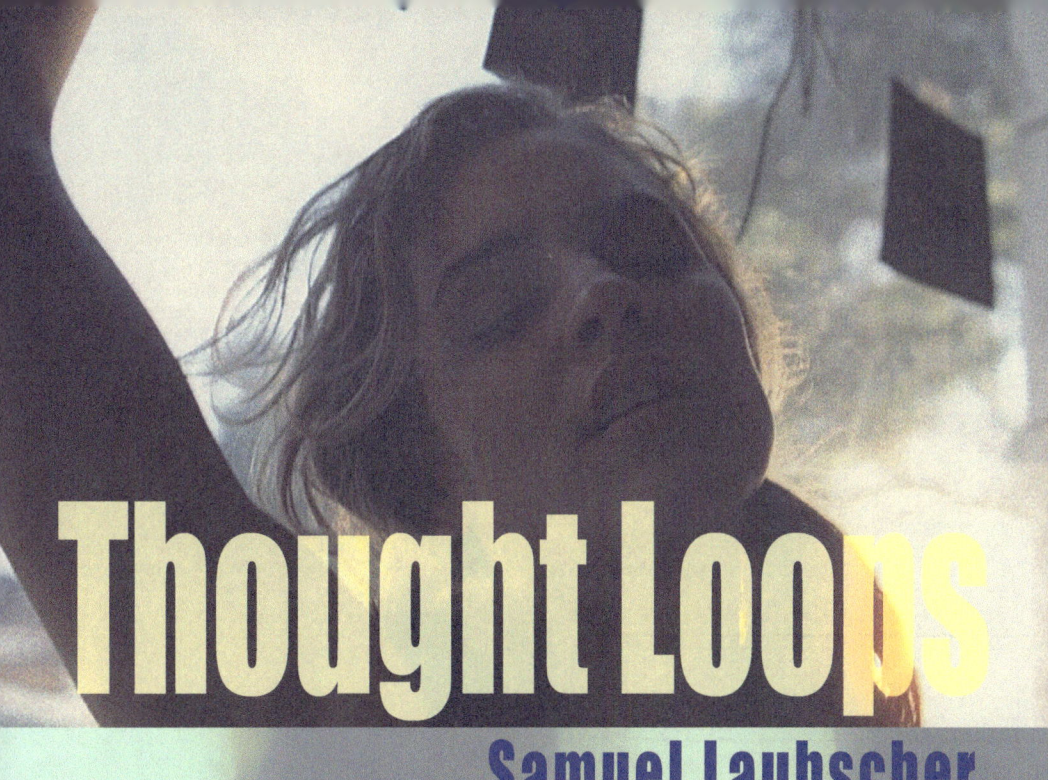

Thought Loops

Samuel Laubscher

Samuel Laubscher is a filmmaker and a musician who creates modern-classical drone compositions under the moniker Hot Air Henry. Son of a British mother (ER Nurse) and an All-American father (Paramedic) who met passing off the injured to each other at a hospital in Los Angeles, California, his early years were spent in the perfect weather of Southern California before he moved out to Atlanta, Georgia. Always holding an interest in photography and motion pictures, Samuel began religiously pursuing the art of the photographic process when he was 15, working solely with 35mm film.

Performed in one long-take and shot on 35mm film, Thought Loops is a collaboration between Samuel/Hot Air Henry and contemporary dancer Erin S Murray. The film is an outpouring which arose from observance of a loved one suffering from the effects of physical depression.

Directed by Samuel Laubscher
Choreographed and performed by Erin S Murray
Gaffer: Kevin Terrell
Key Grip: Bryan Tan
(35mm, Kodak Vision 3 5219, Arriflex 435)

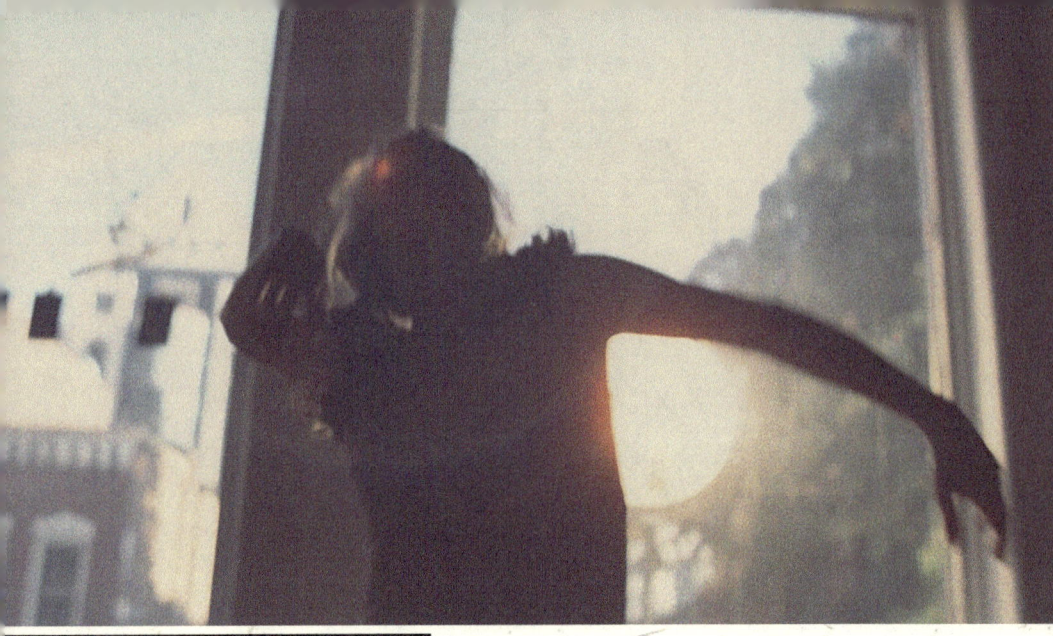

Why 35mm film?

It was my first project I shot on film but I guess in a way I thought to myself maybe *go big or go home*. I really wanted the experience regardless and knew if I wanted to try it out I'd have to create the opportunity for myself, since this was a few years before the film resurgence hit us locally (pre-Kodak Lab Atlanta).

What inspired Thought Loops?

Well, the whole piece is actually quite personal for me. It was sort of a reaction to seeing and helping care for a loved one who was suffering from pretty severe physical depression. I wrote the piece of music for it and as you can tell it is pretty dark. It sort of compounded upon my by own personal struggle so there were many layers to it. But I feel the piece is generally positive. I hoped people would take away an emotion from it that they could hold on to.

How do you balance your musician/filmmaker lives?

A lot of my inspiration is in music, and it's almost my muse to recharge. So sometimes if I'm getting worn out of one art I can shift into the other pretty easily. So it feels more like some weeks i'm a musician and some I'm a cinematographer, but not necessarily both at once, if that makes any sense. More of an emotional place, I suppose. I think one issue that wasn't expecting is that both are careers that require others' consumption. So my forward motion is very based on if I have listeners or people hiring me for my visual style, or essentially the art stops because, well, I run out of money.

How did you and Erin conceptualize choreography?

She had moved to LA fairly recently so I sent her the song and materials and she would send me videos of some phrases she was working on in her studio. I'm not a choreographer by any means so she took on that role as well as performing. When she came in town for the holidays to film we ironed out the rest of the choreography. She is very collaborative in the way in which she works so she would make quite a few suggestions on movement, and even camera placement for some parts, knowing which angles worked best for which movements. She's honestly an amazing artist and I'm so fortunate to have worked with her. She's also a very talented director and I highly suggest people check out her work. My dream is to be hired on one of her projects someday!

This was shot in one take. How did you plan for that?

This was actually pretty fun because there was a touch of celluloid math involved. So the runtime of the song is about 5:40, and I knew from the start I wanted it to be a single take, as if we are part of the choreography and not just on-looking. So a 400' roll of 4-perf would be too short and I didn't have the money or physical strength (I couldn't use an EasyRig because of "the roll", which we talk about below) to operate a 1000' reel the way in which we'd be moving so that was out. But I still wanted to keep a taller frame to be a hair more immersive than the scope of 2-perf (which would again have been too "this is cinema" for me). So, we landed on 3-perf,

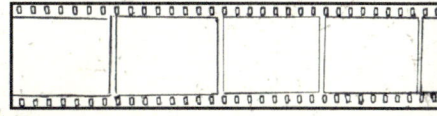

which gave us 5:55 seconds run-time. So was actually a really beautiful thing, we'd literally roll-out just as the performance finished. So we'd be standing there out of breath holding the frame as the last bit of footage was sucked up and the camera would stop speeding. Was quite exhilarating, actually.

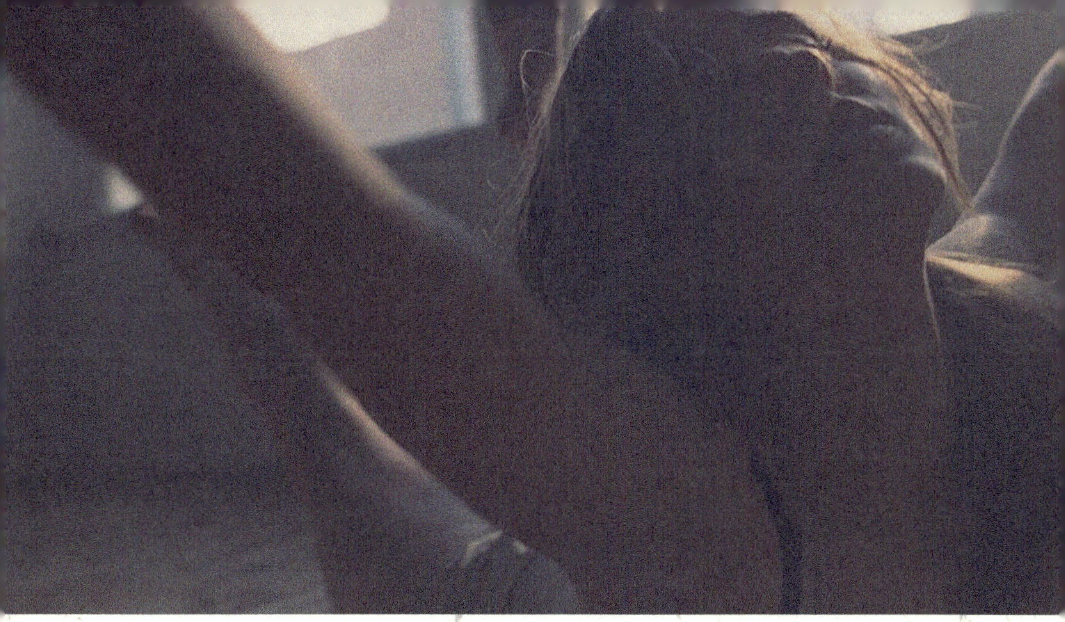

Are you literally rolling around on the floor with a 35mm camera at 4:46?
Ha, pretty much. For that specific moment I started the dutch roll to about 190 degrees and then I passed it of to my key grip, Bryan Tan, who finished the roll and then passed it back to me. Not quite perfect but I think it works for what we were trying to achieve. But the whole thing was such a team effort. We were shooting on the 435 which needed the 24v block batteries, so Bryan was holding that and cable wrangling as Erin and I danced around each other. I definitely was not prepared for the sheer physical workout it would be. We did three takes (not including unloaded camera rehearsals) and both Erin and I were exhausted by the end. But was so much fun, really. Were I to do it again I'd get the stedicam magazines instead of the shoulder ones. Since the take was so long I kept having to shift my grip as the film moved from the front to the back of the magazine, which honestly wore me out more than anything and affected framing at times.

You shot this piece in a DIY venue that no longer exists. How does it feel to have a work of ephemera in a space that was itself ephemeral?

Awe, I know. Was such a beautiful space and they were so accommodating and did so much for the Atlanta arts community. I did hear they are looking to reopen in an old water tower, though!

What advice would you give others wanting to shoot on 35mm for the first time?
At the risk of sounding trite, my advice is to simply do it, create that opportunity for yourself. There is something so fulfilling about shooting celluloid and it's encouraging to get the transfers back and know like 'wow, I do know how to do this. I do use my light meter correctly.' Sometimes digital capture makes me think 'do I actually know what i'm doing or do I just look at the waveform and calibrated monitors until it looks good?' Shooting film removes that doubt and helps remind one that, yes, you can do this.

What's next for you?
I currently have two more dance films in the film festival limbo. They are similar in which they cover aspects mental illness, but each with it's own unique theme. Both filmed in the UK, the first with Rose Alice of the International Arts Collective and the second with Katie James of the Scottish Dance Theatre. I'm very excited about them and hope to release them online as soon as I can.

46

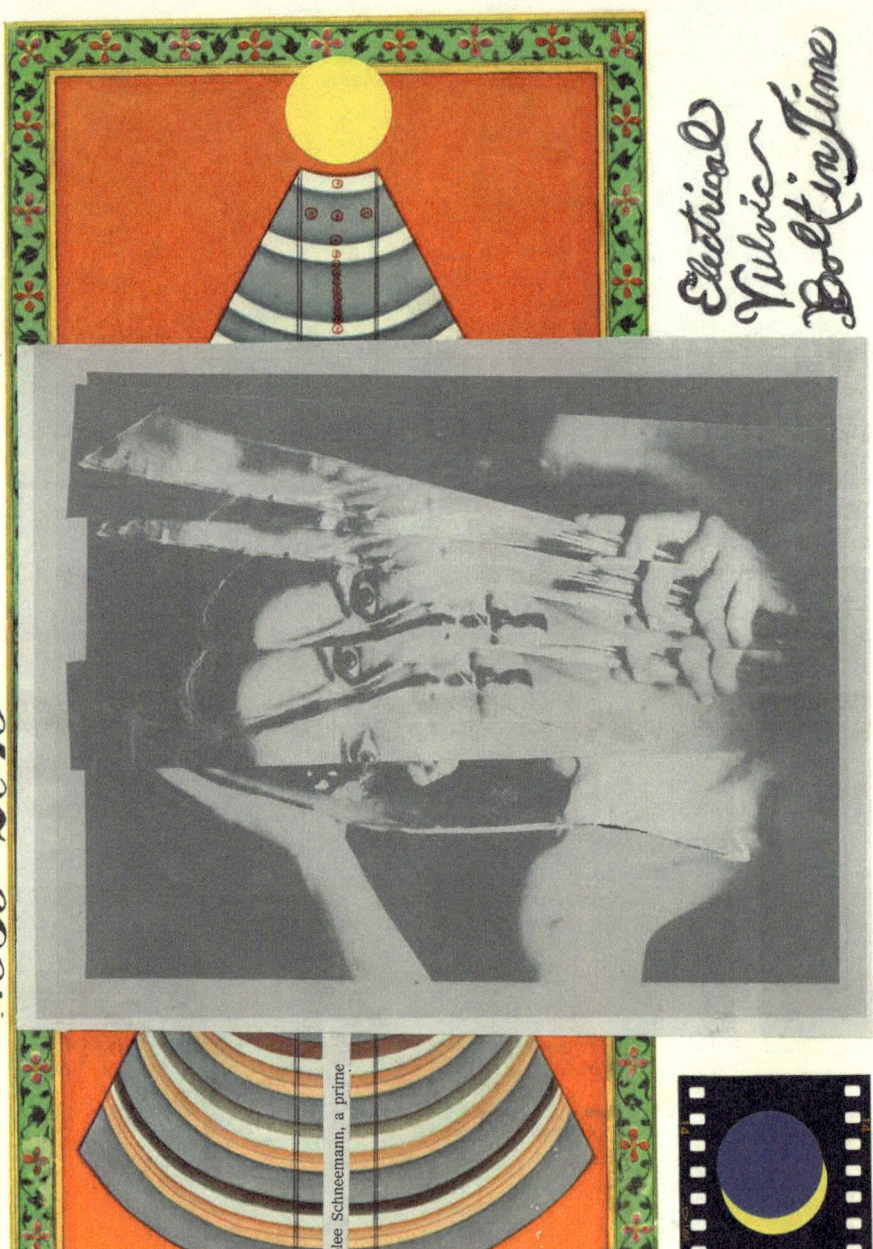

Electrical
Vulvic
Bolt in Time

1939–2019

Carolee Schneemann, a prime

jml

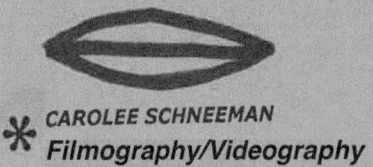

CAROLEE SCHNEEMAN
Filmography/Videography

Viet-Flakes/1962-67

Meat Joy/1964

Fuses/1964-67

Water Light/Water Needle /1966

Body Collage / 1967

Snows/1967-2009

Illinois Central Transposed/1968-69

Plumb Line/1968-71

Kitch's Last Meal/1973-76

Up To And Including Her Limits/ 1974-77

Fresh Blood: A Dream Morphology /1983

Catscan/1990

Ask the Goddess/1991

Vespers Stampede to My Holy Mouth 1992

Is There a Feminist Iconography?/1992

Interior Scroll - The Cave/ 1995

Vulva's School /1995

Known/Unknown—Plague Coumn//1996

Mysteries of the Pussies/1998-2010

Americana I Ching Apple Pie/2007

Infinity Kisses - The Movie/2008

Pinea Silva/2012

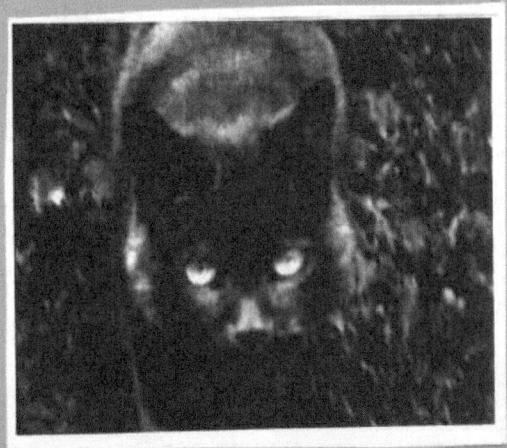

rest in power

Parker Love Bowling

Boudoir
Boudoir
Boudoir

Parker Love Bowling is an actress, writer, and filmmaker from Los Angeles. Based on a series of poems Parker wrote, *Boudoir* is a 16mm film that cuts between ten different girls in their bedrooms and dressing rooms as they have their own dialogue with themselves. When she's not writing and directing, you can catch her in front of the camera and is featured as a Manson girl alongside her sister Kansas Bowling in the Quentin Tarantino film *Once Upon a Time in Hollywood*.

Why film?
Honestly, it just looks better. The colors, the resolution, the grain; it's pretty.

What inspired Boudoir?
I wrote the script after watching Cassavetes' Faces, so one of the characters in Boudoir is inspired by Gena Rowland's character in that film. It was also inspired by the interview sequences in *Masculin Féminin*. Other than that, the film is essentially a compilation of poetry I've written put to images.

Boudoir has an old Hollywood vibe, but it still looks timeless. What inspired the look of the film?
I prefer when films are not set in a specific time period. It's how they withstand the test of time. I did all the art direction myself. The sets and props were made out of stuff I already had laying around my house. I managed to make six different sets out of my sister and I's two bedroom apartment. After wrapping late, I'd have to rearrange all the furniture and set dress a new area, but it was one of my favorite things about working on the film.

In your opinion, what stories are absolutely necessary to tell on celluloid?
I hate it when period pieces are shot digitally. It doesn't look "of the time." But really, I think most everything should be shot on film, especially if one has the budget for it. I'm also working on a documentary right now, but it's shot on an Arri

Alexa Mini because it was equipment already accessible to me without a cost, so I understand it's not always possible.

What's next for you?
I have two feature scripts completed. One is a psychological thriller based on Freudian psychology and the other is a dark romantic comedy. I hope to start production by the end of the year. I also am working on a book of essays, and am of course acting. My first studio film comes out this summer, and my sister's movie that I am in will likely come out by the end of the year. Boudoir is being scored right now, so I'll see what I can do with the film once I have a finished product.

What's one piece of advice you would tell someone shooting on 16mm for the first time?
I would say, make sure you have the budget for an extra role or two of film, because in my experience you always end up shooting more than expected, and it's always good to leave room for spontaneity.

Anything else to add?
I would like to thank my sister, Kansas Bowling and the DP on Boudoir, Andres Garzas for being immensely helpful and patient during my first time shooting analog film, and graciously lending me their equipment. Without them, the film would not have been possible.

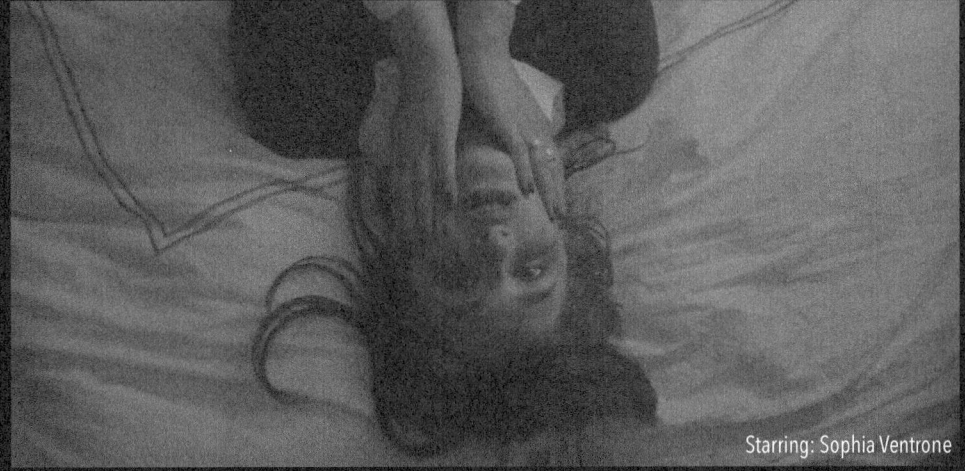

Starring: Sophia Ventrone

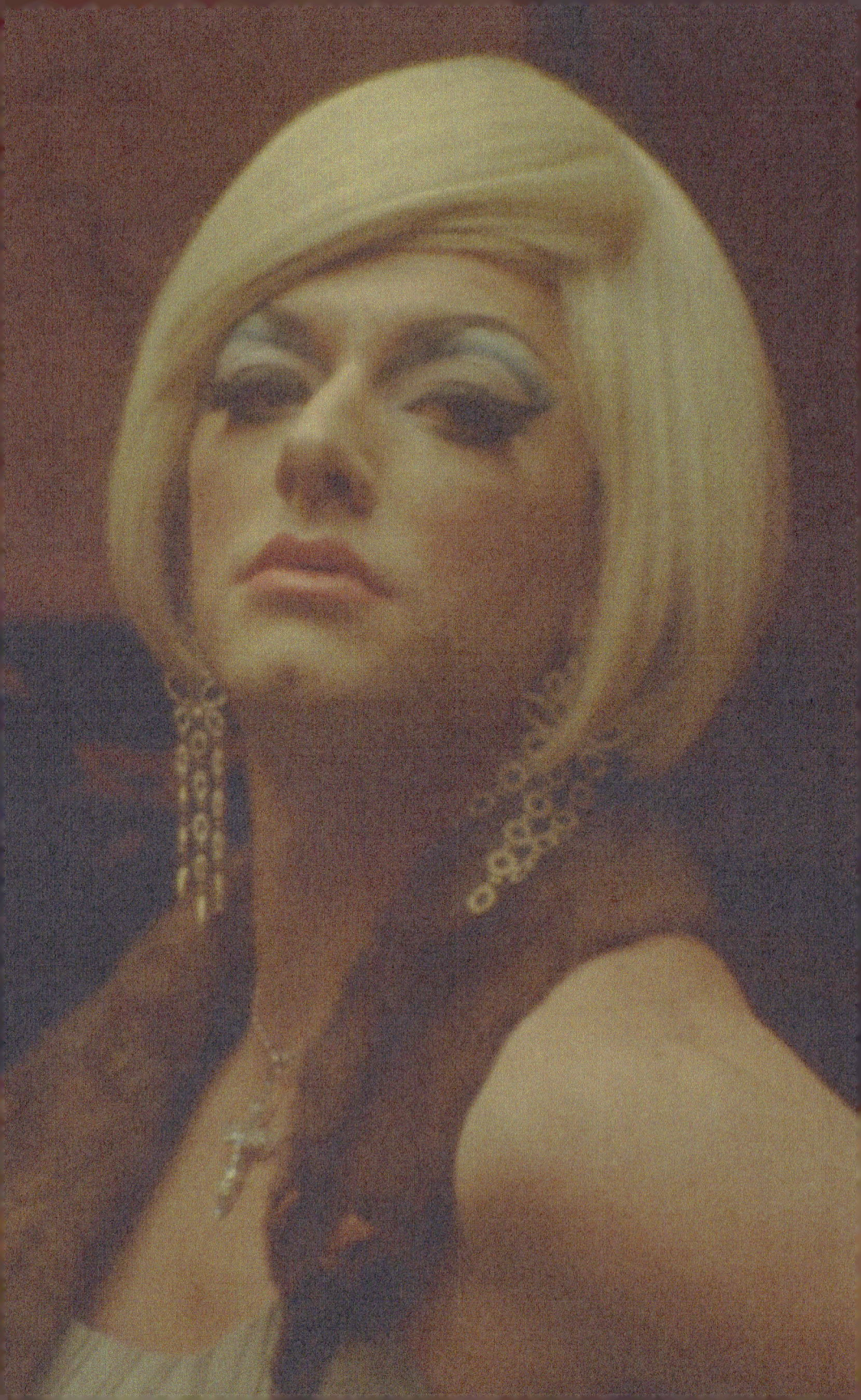

Still of Karen Beaches in *Boudoir*
Directed by Parker Love Bowling
Cinematography by Andres Garzas

Coda MCMLXXXV

Water runs under a bridge
A church looms overhead
A couple films each other on
the shoreline
Walking into a sea of chaotic
filmic decay

Alex Faoro

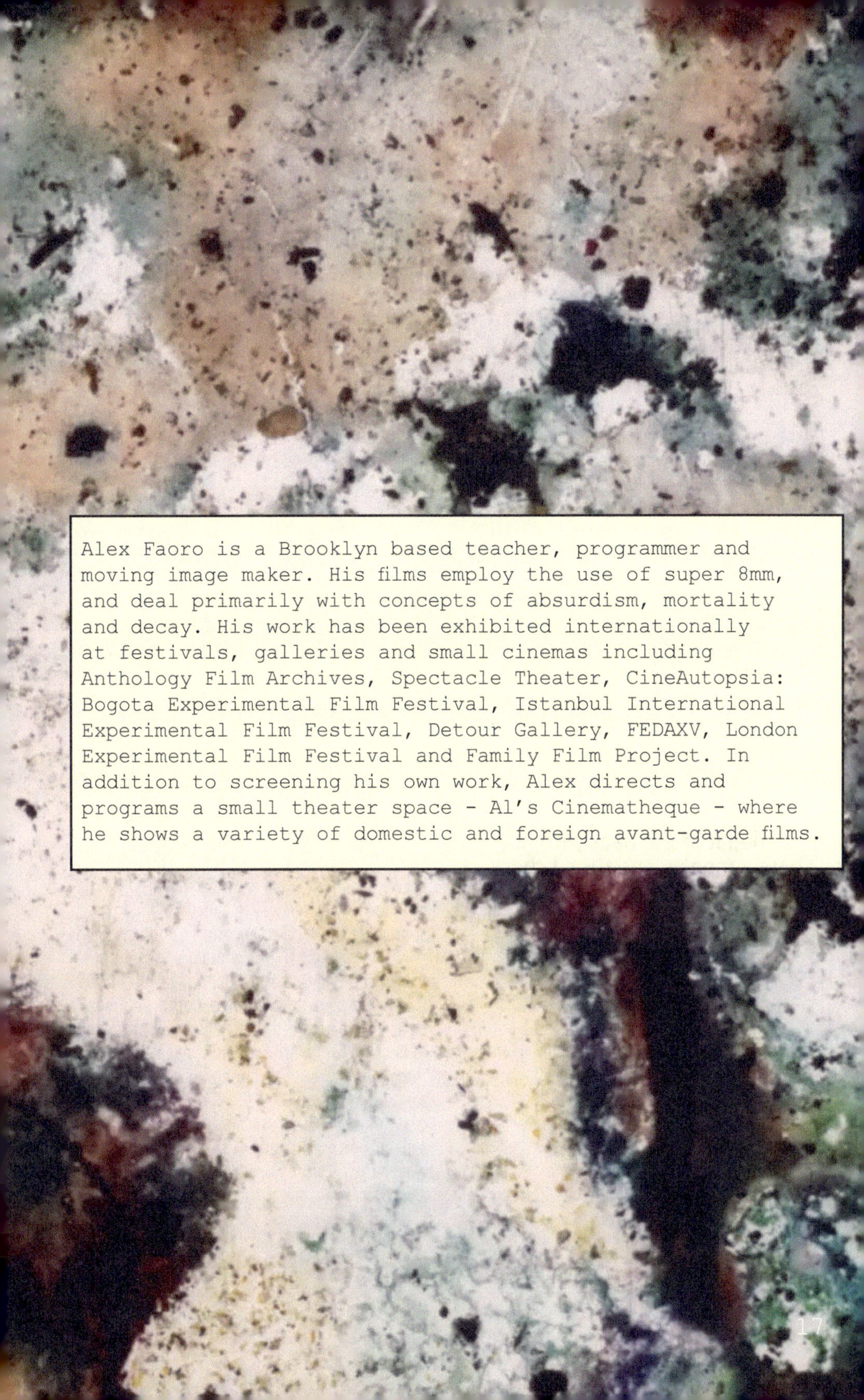

Alex Faoro is a Brooklyn based teacher, programmer and moving image maker. His films employ the use of super 8mm, and deal primarily with concepts of absurdism, mortality and decay. His work has been exhibited internationally at festivals, galleries and small cinemas including Anthology Film Archives, Spectacle Theater, CineAutopsia: Bogota Experimental Film Festival, Istanbul International Experimental Film Festival, Detour Gallery, FEDAXV, London Experimental Film Festival and Family Film Project. In addition to screening his own work, Alex directs and programs a small theater space - Al's Cinematheque - where he shows a variety of domestic and foreign avant-garde films.

What do you do?

Right now, I currently teach photography and filmmaking in New York City public schools through a number of organizations. That's kind of my bread and butter for making money. In terms of my filmmaking, my interest has always been in things that are autobiographical, intimate, or personal. I grew up on classic Hollywood films at my grandmother's place, and then was trained formally in documentary, but in the past two or three years, found my way into experimental cinema.

I've been exploring themes of home, memory, and family, but doing it in more obscured or abstracted ways without the use of narrative and with the use of small format celluloid. I think along with my interest in those themes comes an interest in things like Super 8, and videotape, and all the home movie formats that people have used over the years to capture those intimate moments.
What's the correct pronunciation of Coda?
You can do the whole Roman numeral thing, but it's 1985. It was the year that my dad and my mom shot that film, so it's a more elegant way to write the numbers than just the actual numbers.

Where did the idea of repurposing your parents' footage come from?

"I buried it in the back yard, for about a month, and then I checked it periodically. As I saw the results, I began to become more intrigued in what had been filmed, and what was happening to the film. "

I came across the footage haphazardly. Every time I go home ... My family lives in New Jersey, although they're from Brooklyn. My grandmother still lives there. My dad lives with her, my cousin lives with her, and so I find that her house and my dad's old place, across the yard, were treasure troves for weird, old things that you could find. So, every time I go home, I kind of just go into the garage and start rummaging through things.
My dad was a photographer and filmmaker, so I find a lot of his old things there. Both of my grandparents worked for the Army, at some point. There's a lot of papers, old photos, and all sorts of relics that I dust off. For a while I was actually looking for a bunch of Regular-8mm home movies that my family had spoken of as if it was mythology. "Oh, these are here, but we don't know where they are." So I always kind of looked for them.

In that process, I came across another reel of film. It's probably about four- or five-hundred feet, with a big, full reel, and I don't think anybody had watched it, as with a lot of these home movies--no one ever really watches them, for some reason.

Was there one filmmaker, in particular, that inspired you to bury it?

There is, although he didn't do burial work. I was interested in the materialistic and thematic idea of decay. And that's something that I explored in one of my earlier Super 8 films called *The Melody of Decomposition*. It's not buried, but it's the idea for mortality and decay, family and home, and things like that.

I went to Anthology Film Archives in New York and I met Stephen Broomer, who's a filmmaker in Toronto. I stayed in contact with him, and he would give me some recipes for different chemistry to do mordançage solution. The idea of manipulating the film was interesting to me. But doing the whole Mordançage thing became a lot to do, and I wasn't certain if I had all the resources. I was thinking of another way to affect the film in a somewhat similar fashion, and I landed on burying it. I hadn't done it before, and I didn't really have any connection to that film, specifically. I buried it in the back yard, for about a month, and then I checked it periodically. As I saw the results, I began to become more intrigued in what had been filmed, and what was happening to the film. And it was sort of fortuitous that it continued that thread of themes that I was exploring. It's a somewhat organic process, in and of itself, and finding my way there.

The pacing is very interesting. At certain points the film freezes on one frame, and then it will speed up again. How did you decide the pacing?

It's funny because a lot of these decisions come from non decisions. I have a Eumich Mark 607-D projector, which has all these different frame rates that you can project at, and one of my friends saw the film and she wanted to program it. I was showing the original print at Spectacle Theater for the first time and the projector was not working properly, so I had to stand in the back and hold the gate shut and tinker with it as the film was going through. It was a performance, to some degree, and so there were moments where the film would get stuck, at the gate, and it would burn a little bit of the image, and I thought, that's not what I wanted to happen. But, anyway, it happened. After the screening, some folks came up to me and said, "I really liked the moments when I get to see your mom's face, or I get to read the detail, and the granules, and the dirt." When I went back to edit it, I thought about that. I thought about giving the audience an opportunity to inspect some of these frames, some of which are pretty intricate.

On the subject of screening at Spectacle, and different places: Do you have a favorite place that you have screened your work?
Honestly, my favorite place to screen my work is in my apartment. I do a lot of programming at my apartment, which is tentatively called Al's Cinematheque, and I think it coincides with what I'm interested in with my films, the idea of showing films at home, and bringing it outside of the pre-established venue that's created for film. That's not to say that I don't enjoy showing at the galleries, or festivals, but there's something about it being in somebody's home, and there's something about the space where you're contextualizing the art itself.

Both Coda and "The Melody of Decomposition" are silent. Do you always work without sound?
I guess it's a purist way of thinking. For some reason, it just makes sense to me. My family made a lot of home movies, so when I watch these old home movies, it's always silent. There's no musical accompaniment, or dialogue, or anything. It just feels like I'm retaining a similar cultural quality about it. That's the explanation I've used to justify it, so far, but it could change. Some of my more recent things have sound, but they're also on videotape, and that can record sound. Maybe those two things will merge, at some point.

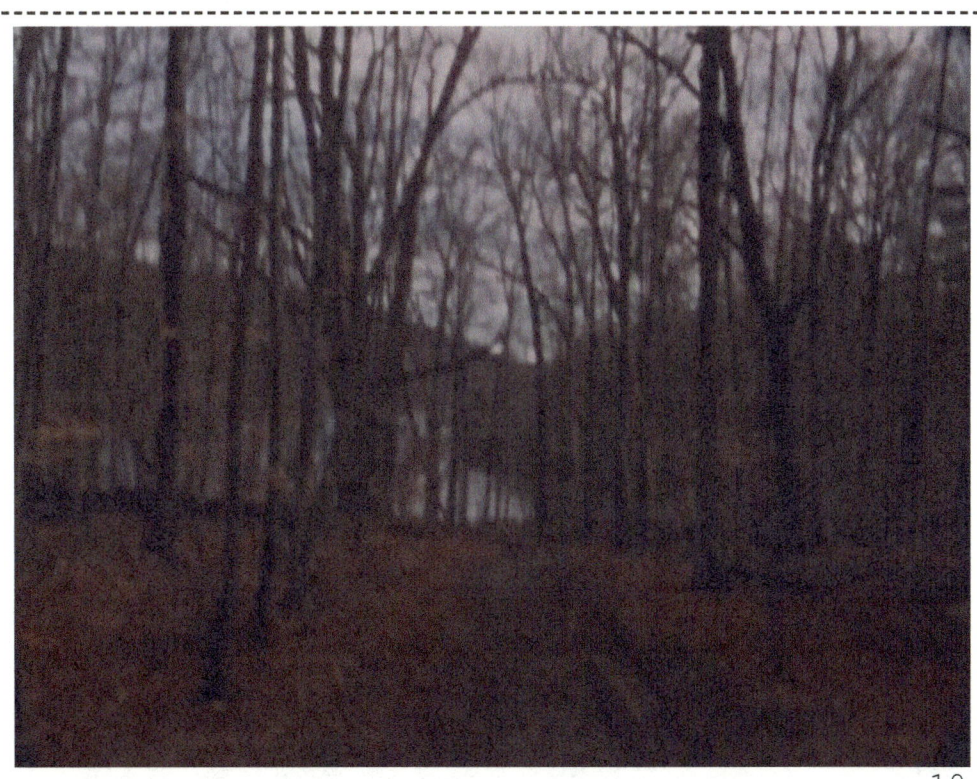

Thoughts on SMALL Filmmaking

On March 16th I organized a screening of 8mm experimental films at my apartment in North Brooklyn, a space aptly called Al's Cinematheque. The program showcased a number of contemporary artists who work with 8mm small format in a variety of ways. This includes direct-filmmaking, organic decay, impressionistic shooting methods and other formal modes of experimentation. In addition to their respective practices, these individuals have also preserved a particular philosophy of filmmaking, one I've attempted to elucidate below.

Sunday, Monday and Tuesday I was out of film in Chicago - Erica Sheu (USA | 2019)
Retracing Home - Karissa Hahn (USA | 2013)
Sketch Film #4 - Tomonari Nishikawa (USA | 2007)
Midway - Dan Browne (Canada | 2008)
DFidédente - Annalisa D. Quagliata (Mexico | 2016) *Coda MCMLXXXV* - Alex Faoro (USA | 2018)
Starfish Aorta Colossus - Lynne Sachs (USA | 2015)
Anche in paradiso non è bello essere soli - Lorenzo Gattorna (Italy/USA | 2017)

Since its conception in 1932, 8mm film – in all its forms – has possessed a certain alluring quality, one that's inspired multiple generations of *amateurs filmmakers*. I say *amateur* to point out the fact that very few of these artists, if any, go on to make even a cent from their work.

Rather, their films are not motivated by financial pursuit in the first place. They're pure quotidian remarks, used to shape the creative reality of those who make them. I suppose this is what originally enthralled me about the small format - the uninhibited manner with which you could point your camera at something and begin filming, almost unconsciously. Speaking for myself, the result (of filming) is only subsidiary to the ecstatic experience of wielding a camera and producing a series of ostensibly random yet important images. I interpret this act to be a sort of anarchic visual declaration, one in which the artist seeks to establish a new visual language. Displeased with convention and displaced by the ubiquity of modern commercial images, they attempt to re-conceptualize the unique metaphysical qualities of *home*.

In my view, *home* can be best understood as a way of defining oneself in relation to the rest of the world. By this I mean, it's an essential condition that dictates how we comprehend our individual existence and communicate our distinctive experiences to others. Consequently, *home* always strikes me as an intrinsic aspect of self-expression and relation.

Home Movie: A short amateur film or video made to preserve a visual record, typically intended for viewing at home by family and friends

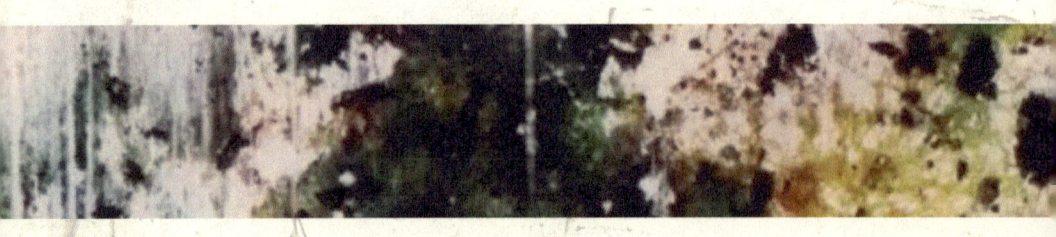

The 8mm format has always been inextricably linked to the phenomenon of *home movie-making*. And the films listed above are notable examples of this enduring custom. Moreover, they each implement their own unique approach to the cultural practice. For example, in my own film, *Coda MCMLXXXV*, I use burial and exhumation as a means of distorting images that my parents made thirty year prior while on a brief trip in Rhode Island. In doing so, I attempt to highlight the interrelationship between memory, decay and materialism - themes consistent in my early work. Similar to my film, Lorenzo Gattorna's *Anche in paradiso non è bello essere soli* celebrates the indiscriminate result of organic decay. As we watch his family live and die in the   old country, blue crystalline-like water damage jumps eloquently across the screen. Using more deliberative interventionist tools like bleach and paint, Karissa Hahn's *Retracing Home* abstracts representational imagery in order to create a colorful and synaptic rhythm, one that offers only brief glimpses of a blue splattered garden.

Using a markedly different approach, Dan Browne and Tomonari Nishikawa employ in-camera editing techniques to transform their environments. In *Midway*, Browne's camera paints the sky with the circulating and flickering machines of the Canadian National Exhibition, abstracting their luminescent forms in beautiful refractive patterns. Nishikawa on the other hand uses single frame animation to construct *Sketch Film #4*. Utilizing everyday shapes and colors, he creates mesmerizing geometric grids that move fluidly across the screen.

Erica Sheu's travelogue, *Sunday, Monday and Tuesday I was out of film in Chicago*, uses expired Ektachrome G and black & white film to explore her prospective new home. Looking through Federico Herrero's colorful installation at the Museum of Contemporary Art Chicago, Sheu contemplates how she might interpret the city's unfamiliar landscape. In *Starfish Aorta Colossus* Lynne Sachs demonstrates the effect of parallel imagery and simple utterances. Using Paolo Javier's writing and her own revisited double 8mm films, she establishes lyrical connections between seemingly disparate words and memories. Annalisa D. Quagliata also uses spoken- word to frame her grainy black & white snapshots of Mexico City in *DFiédente*. Using this dialogue, she reflects on her native city, its people and history. In doing so, she beckons her audience to listen closely to her desirous whispers for change…

All of these films possess intimate qualities of their makers' psyches and habitats. These elements take shape tangibly and metaphysically, establishing a unique language through which each filmmaker's process of creation consecrates his, her, or their respective notions of *home*. This is the anarchic visual declaration I earlier identified - a process in which everyone's inventive energy populates an unending spectrum of creative realities.

To that end, I propose we advance the *amateur* philosophy in a more comprehensive fashion. Drawing on the influence of 8mm, yet not limited by the medium itself, we ought to reconstitute the platform for *small filmmaking*. More people ought to make personal films, not in order to dismiss social, political, or economic realities, but rather to present them in a manner that supersedes the remote gaze of impassivity. In doing so, we might encounter and successfully redefine the syntactic boundaries of cinematic language… thereby creating a new *home*.

-Alex Faoro

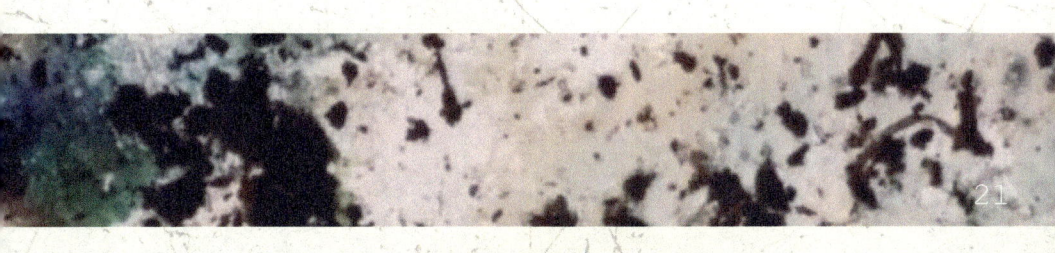

me comí
un ostión
y luego
me comí
tu corazón

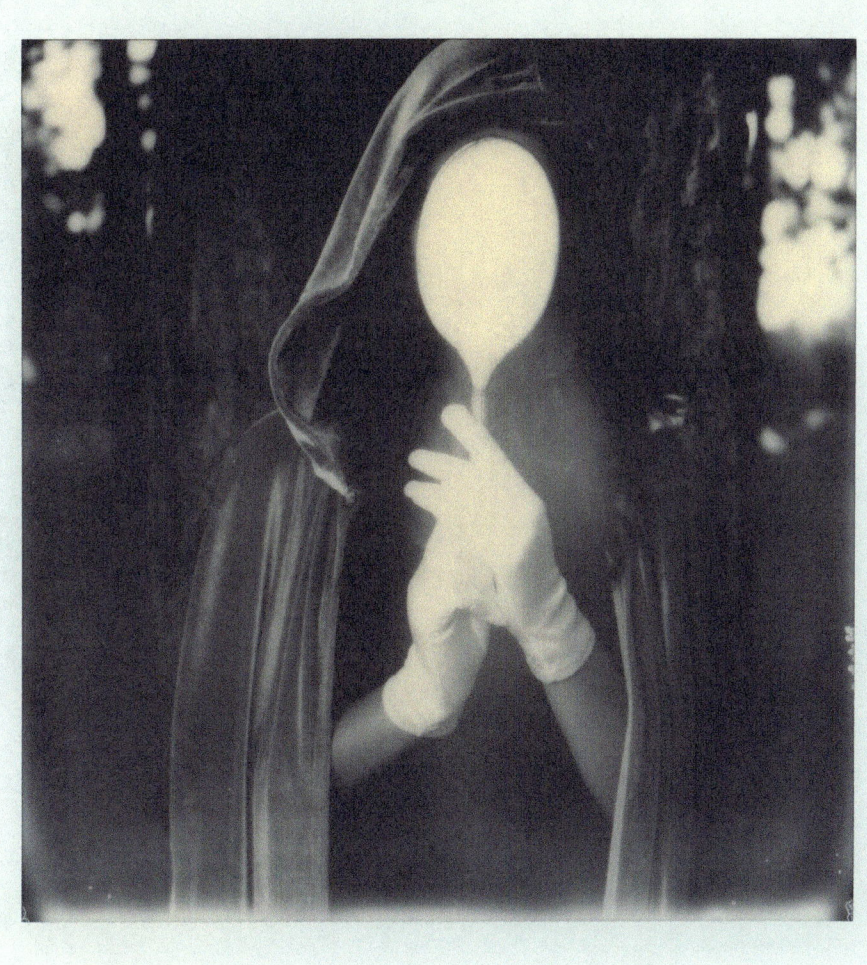

ShesaidRed

Shesaidred

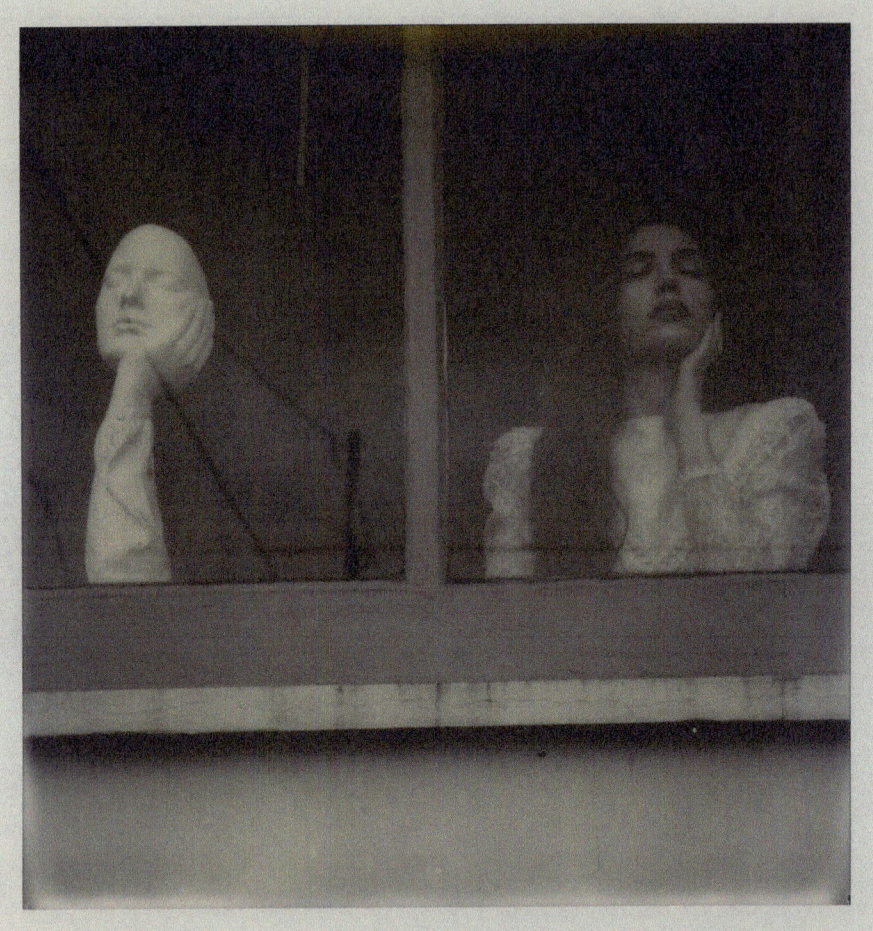

photographer/filmmaker/artist

Shesaidred (né Norma Córdova) is a photographer, filmmaker, and artist born and raised in Oregon by hardworking Mexican immigrant parents. She is currently living in the bay area where she works for the Lawyer's Committee for Civil Rights and Labor Commissioner of San Francisco.

She happened upon photography unexpectedly. "I fell into photography by taking an elective class in junior college and that changed the trajectory," she said. "I really was fascinated when I was taking biology class by looking at the microscope and seeing things go into motion." From that point on, she was hooked. "It was like an addiction for me. Watching that latent image just appear magically through the development, I was just like so floored."

Twenty years later, Shesaidred has built a portfolio of works that explores feminine dream-like spaces. In her ongoing project Mood, Memory, Myth, she explores "moody narratives, evoking fear, anxiety, and pleasure," and notes on her website that, "the simple of acts of photographing those subjects helps her explore her inner desires and what her Mexican culture and family expected of her as a female: to wed and have children." The photographic result is black and white and sepia toned images that have been manipulated in the dark room and painted on to distort and call attention to other worlds that exist beneath the surface.

About this process, Shesaidred said "I would actually load black and white fiber paper into my holders and shoot. Then I would take those paper negatives into the dark room. They're negatives so I would enlarge and then distress them afterwards. What's interesting is I print in the color dark room. I do the toning through the color dark room. I use filtration through it and I also utilize rejected and expired photographic paper."

She decided to move into moving image and created *Un Ostion* (The Oyster in English), a 16mm film she shot on a Bolex through a course at the Northwest Film Center in Portland, Oregon. In it, she presents a visual poem that explores an internal dream world as the protagonist comes

into contact with a more sinister version of herself. She casted actress Ana Corbi to play the lead and together they collaborated to craft a mysterious character. "It spoke to us about the femininity, the duality that lives within women and how the conflict that exists within us about our sexuality and those conflicts around our it." The result is a film that feels both familiar and foreign as if the audience is in a dream along with the protagonist.

She notes that Un Ostion was, like all of her analog projects, a love project. "It's the unknown and that unplanned part of it that is still really captivates me. I don't want to know everything." With all of her work, Shesaidred fearlessly and relentless explores the unknown and creates photos and films that feels like acts of self-love. She leaves me with a phrase: *me comí un ostión y luego me comí tu corazón*. It roughly translates to "I ate an oyster and then I ate your heart," but a non literal translation could be "I consumed the world and then devoured your heart."

"It's like an ode to myself," she said. "I ate the oyster. I ate the world, then I ate my own heart."

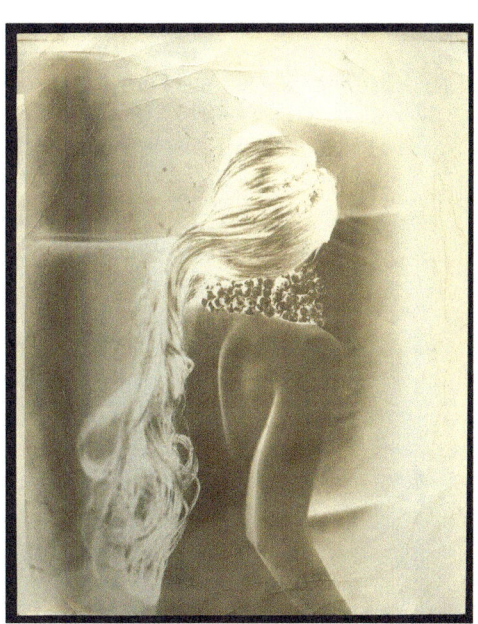

THE AATON LTR

BY KANSAS BOWLING

+ an Angénieux lens!

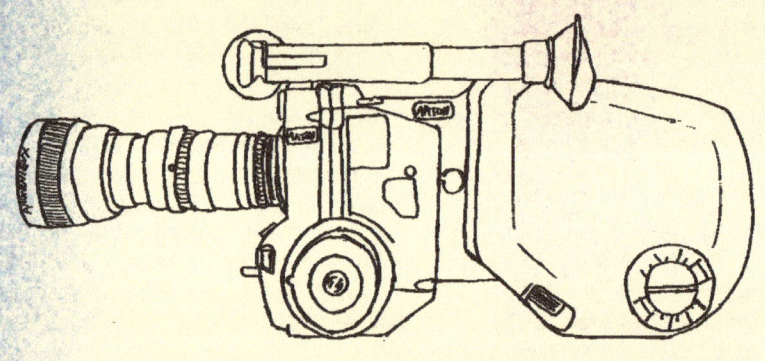

The Aaton LTR is by far my favorite camera I've ever shot with! My first feature B.C. Butcher was shot on an Arriflex SRII with a $20,000 lens or something fancy like that. And it looked like 35mm! But I was shooting 16mm because I wanted it to look like 16mm! I've shot many things on various super 8 cameras and wind-up Bolex-style 16mm cameras, but for my second feature (coming soon!) I was lucky enough to find the camera I will be sticking with for the rest of my career! The Aaton LTR paired with my Angénieux 12-120 lens shoots 16mm the way 16mm should always look — sharp and cinematic, but with enough grain and the occasional (beautiful) scratch to remind you of the images' tangibility. But when shooting with an old camera (though this one is younger than you would think — late 70s) there are bound to be the occasional problems that instructional manuals can't always help you with. And the internet has maybe only one or two forums dedicated to the entire camera! So for the few people out there currently shooting with an Aaton LTR — here are some very specific tips to the camera and some solutions to problems I've encountered!

1 A tip for choosing film stocks: I've come to find that 50D, 250D, and 200T of the Kodak stocks shoot BEAUTIFULLY on the camera — but not so much the 500T. I've shot some great things on 500T on other cameras but for some reason it doesn't react best with the XTR. When I do shoot with it though (which is actually often → I've gotten so many 500T donations!) I treat it like expired film and slightly overexpose.

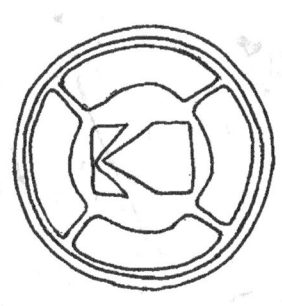

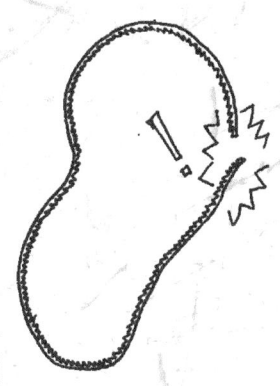

2 This is a very quiet camera! Which is so wonderful. But if it's not quiet, it's trying to tell you something is up. A camera that speaks to you!!! If you find that its super loud when it is rolling, make sure the film isn't too tightly wound and there is enough space to fit two three fingers in the loop sticking outside the magazine. If there isn't, you could get back some streaked footage! Lost loops look cool sometimes, but I've never been disappointed getting footage back and seeing one. If you intentionally want streaked footage — load the film TIGHT!

3 The rubber belt inside the magazine that catches onto the film's sprockets is extremely delicate. The rest of the camera is a tank but this tiny piece has broken in all three of my magazines just from wear! Luckily I live in Hollywood and near Abel Cine who are the actual Anton specialists! Each time they have broke they've been able to hunt down these rare pieces for me and replaced them for cheap!

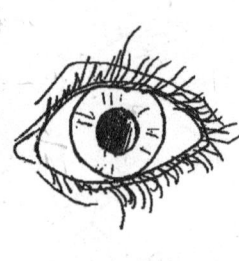

4 The Angénieux lens—which I believe was commonly paired with the LTR shoots GORGEOUSLY—but I would avoid using it for wide shots. The 12-120 is at it's best when shooting at medium and close-up (though not macro) and the zoom on it is incredible. I'd recommend getting a wide lens as well as the zoom (though I don't even have one yet—just want one!!!) if you're shooting with this same camera package!

5 One time my lens was suddenly not focusing and I had to end a shoot early! I was panicked, thinking I'd have to spend hundreds on a repair, but it turns out there was just a small screw in the lens that needed to be tightened! Everything in this camera makes perfect sense in how it operates, even to a non-engineer or even camera person. When something breaks, it's often such a simple fix, you can tell what needs to be done just by looking at it!

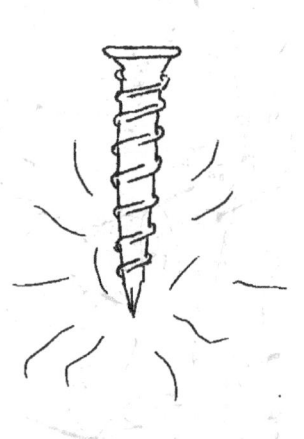

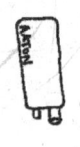
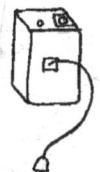

6 For a short time, the battery was wiggly and would sometimes lose it's power unless it was held in place. I took it in for repair and they just had to reline the rubber holes connecting the battery to the camera! Not even an electrical issue! And by the way— these batteries may have to charge 5-6 hours before shooting (which I have stress-dreams often where I forget to plug them in) on a battery charger that looks like a bomb (TSA hates me) but they can shoot 10 ROLLS without having to be swapped out for a new battery!

The Aaton LTR is most importantly an entirely durable camera. It's gone through a helluva lot being owned by me, constantly being taken on planes and being flown around the world — shooting at the beach, in the jungle, and in the literal 125° desert. She can stand it! She's not extremely heavy for nothing!

As a bonus - here are some of my signiture human tripod poses!

Leaning it on my hip!

Moving your knee while the camera rests on it has a dolly effect!

HOPE THIS CAN HELP ONE OR TWO PEOPLE!

Thank you Andres Garzas for teaching me how to shoot 16mm!

Thank you Don De Vore for always carrying the camera for me between takes!

Thank you Tim Pronovost for (permanently) loaning me the camera in the first place!

E6 processing & Ektachrome

E6 - Color Reversal Process Instructions

1. Prewash: 1 minute (use warm water)
2. 1st Developer: 6.5 minutes @ 105 degrees F
3. Wash- Fill and empty the tank 7 times with warm water
4. Color Developer: 4.5 minutes @ 105 degrees F
5. Wash- Fill and empty the tank 7 times with warm water
6. Blix: 10 minutes @ 80-105 degrees F
7. Final Wash: 5 minutes
8. Photoflow
9. Hang to dry

Ektachrome is a color reversal stock by Kodak that contains over 80 ingredients to produce beautiful, saturated images. What's great about this stock is it is relatively easy to process on your own compared to other color stocks that can get complicated fast. It's available on 35mm still, super 8, and most recently 16mm. If you're shooting on super 8 or 16mm, you can use a lomo tank designed specifically for super 8 and 16mm film for precision, or keep it cheap and shove all your film into a 35mm tank like spaghetti.

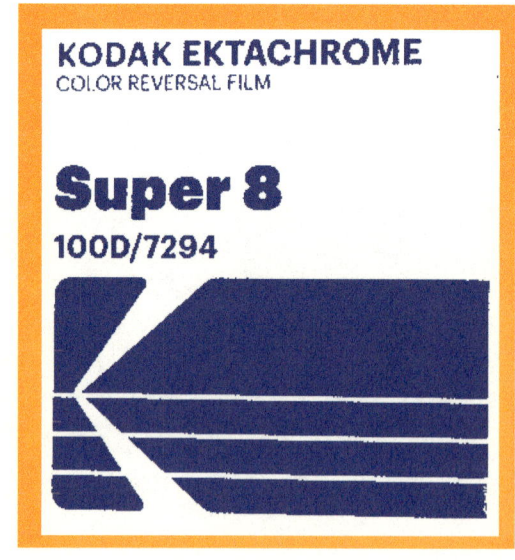

KODAK EKTACHROME
COLOR REVERSAL FILM

Super 8
100D/7294

THE CINE-VINYL RECORD-JECTOR

WITH SALLY CINNAMON

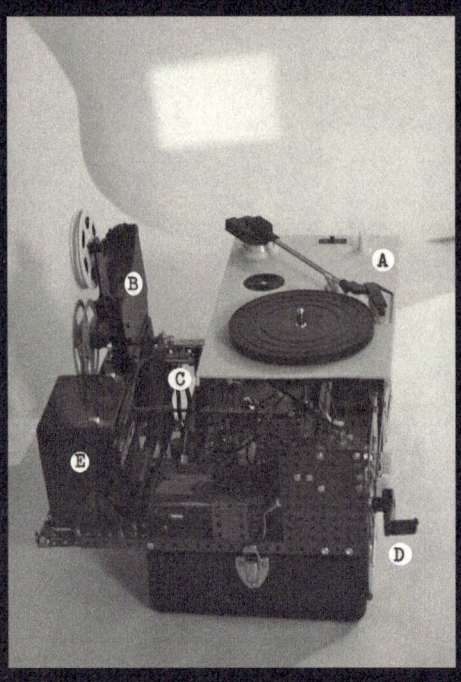

The
CINEVINYL
RECORDJECTOR

Figure A
Modified Crosley CR40 Mini Turntable

Figure B
Modified Gakken Super 8 Mini-Projector

Figure C
Gear assembly syncing turntable rotation
with takeup reel rotation

Figure D
Hand-wound power, just like the earliest
record players and projectors

Figure E
Battery power supply for portability

OVER

AND

OUT

SUPER
WIND 7 / 8 ·UP
CINEVINYL

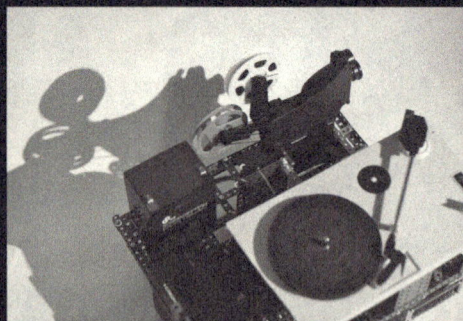

RECORDJECTOR

your turntable's not dead
and neither is your projector

Bands shot by OVER AND OUT Films on super 8
include:

THE KILLS

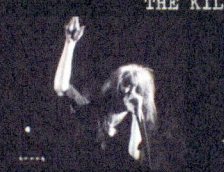
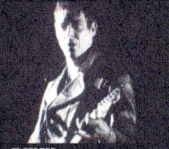

HUNX AND HIS PUNX

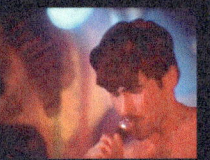
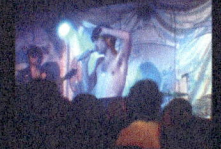

THE RACONTEURS

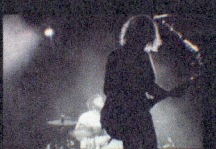
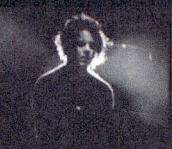

s well as JEFF the Brotherhood, The Black
lles, Black Milk, The Dirtbombs, Thee Oh Sees,
and more.

Seven inch records and super 8 film are
analog, and analogous.
They both offer tangible experiences that
are beautiful, immediate, and limited.
Seven inch records hold less than ten
minutes of music per side.
Super 8 film reels are three minutes each,
more when spliced together.
Super 8 film has always been the DIY film
format - from family home movies in the
1960s and 1970s (cousin of the wholesome
mass-marketed 45) to the most obscure
guerrilla filmmaking and student experimentation (cousin to the cheap punk seven
inch) today.
These daze, music videos are treated as
disposable - lost in an endless sea of
competition with millions of internet
videos, tightly compressed in scale for
viewing on telephones of all things, and
squeezed into rarer and rarer airtime on
television.
    But music videos

are special   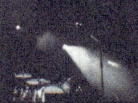   and important.

The SUPER 7/8 WIND-UP CINEVINYL RECORDJECTOR
is a combined RECORD PLAYER and PROJECTOR
for 7" records and super 8 reels of film.

It is the ONLY combined vinyl record player
and motion picture film projector IN HISTORY.

Many people now agree that there is something
about vinyl records that makes the experience
of buying, owning, and listening to them
valuable in a way that mp3s and cds cannot.

The experience of watching film be wound
and projected through light onto a screen,
wall, or even ceiling is special in a way
that digital video on a television or
computer can never be.

Film is widely seen as UNAVAILABLE - unless
you're very old or maybe in film school -
UNSUSTAINABLE - for filmmakers at the mercy
of youtubers of all ages - IRRELEVANT -
why buy the film when you can get the app
for free?' - and DEAD.

Vinyl's been there. Vinyl has come back.

Film can too.

All OVER AND OUT concert footage is shot on
super 8 film from the audience with cameras
variously smuggled in, confiscated, and
tolerated.
OVER AND OUT always attempts to obtain
permission from the performers when possible
OVER AND OUT Films is currently undergoing
conversion to all manual editing,with plans
to expand into a private laboratory for
internal film processing within the year.
OVER AND OUT Films is the owner and pro-
prietor of ONE of only THREE SUPER 8
OPTICAL PRINTERS in North America - the
only machine that can print copies of
super 8 films on super 8.

Sally Cinnamon is the 21 year old filmmaker
and inventor behind OVER AND OUT Films. Her
first super 8 film, Little Red Bill, has
screened in festivals in Washington DC,
New York, Brooklyn, and Toronto. Under
another name, she has also been a scholarship winner, ballet dancer, circus performe:
and published writer. Sally also plays drum
in The Cool Hands, with whom she has released two 7" records.

headquarters@overandoutfilms.com

33

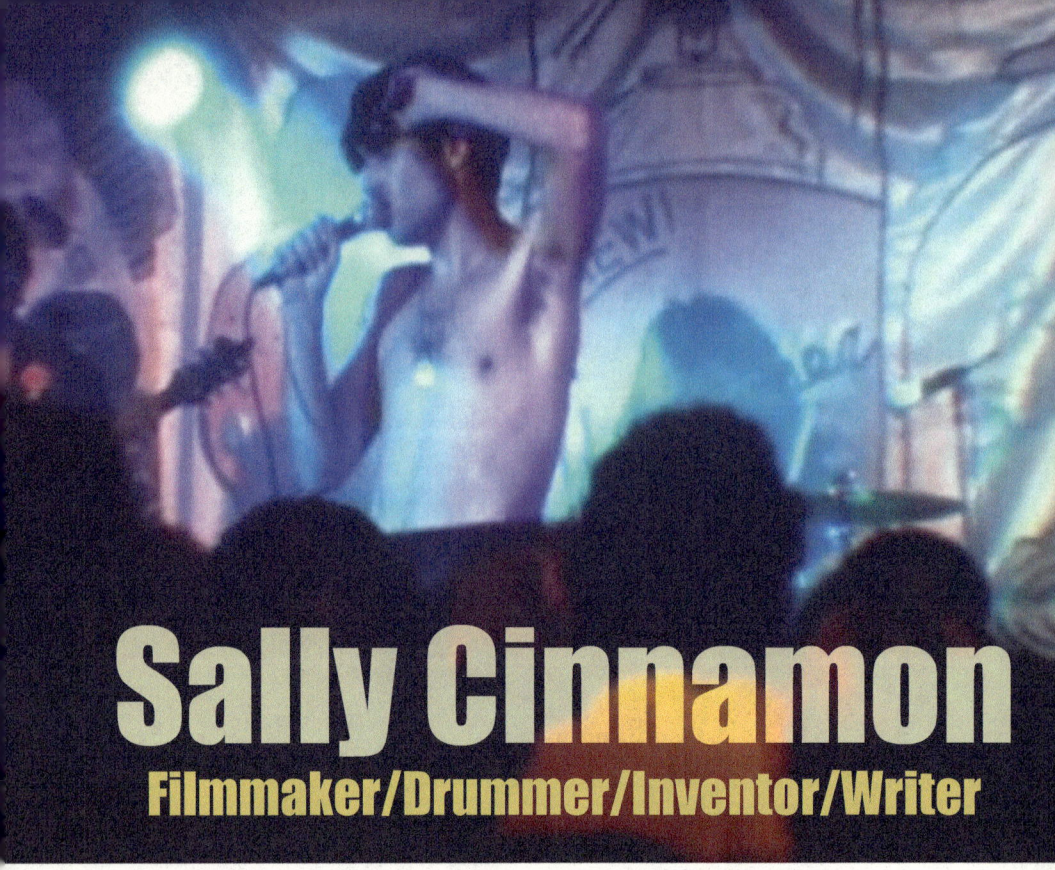

Sally Cinnamon
Filmmaker/Drummer/Inventor/Writer

Sally Walker-Hudecki (AKA Sally Cinnamon) is a jane of all trades from Toronto where she currently works at Yowza Animation--the largest solely female owned animation studio in the world. She also writes compulsively, studies at University of Toronto, and plays in the band the Cool Hands where she has released several vinyl records and played with bands like La Luz and FIDLAR. When she's not drumming, writing, or working, she can be found making super 8mm live music videos at shows or working on her invention the Cinevinyl recordjector--the only machine in the world that syncs vinyl to super 8mm films.

How did you get into making super 8 music videos?
I've made videos my whole life on all kinds of formats: webcam first, VHS, digital video (mini-dv). I read about super 8 in the seminal text: GIRL DIRECTOR: A How-To Guide for the First Time, Flat Broke Film and Video Maker. I thought, haven't tried that. So I took a super 8 workshop at Hart House at University of Toronto in 2010. The test film I shot for that class went into festivals.

In high school I was diagnosed with temporal lobe epilepsy, which made me feel like a freak of nature. Because of epilepsy, I was always sober at shows, so I started taking pictures of bands, to keep my hands busy. I went to Nashville in 2011 to see JEFF the Brotherhood and to celebrate some independence from my illness. I brought a super 8 camera and capturing their performance on film felt like magic.

The circumstances were such that I could continue to travel and film bands in Toronto and elsewhere throughout my early 20s, making over 20 finished, edited, live super 8 music videos - some guerilla, some officially. I went to Nashville, Memphis, St. Louis, NYC, London, Olympia, Detroit, Montreal, and on a cruise ship from Miami - Nassau. I filmed bands in locations that were relevant to their careers. I am putting together a screening for these in the next 2 months at Niagara Custom Lab.

Why super 8?
I think it's more beautiful than most other motion imaging. It captures the way I see things when I feel something. There is a dialogue about digital vs. analog that focuses on external factors, creating philosophical or moral stances about physicality, economics, and limitations, but really, I use super 8

because it's beautiful and hard to get, like me. I love the way light looks on film, I love that the reels end and I can't have it right away, and I love the smell.

What's your favorite music video you've made so far?

So hard to choose! Stop it! I love my most recent work: "I'm On" for CATL, which was the first time I got to try collaging super 8 on top of digital video to fill up the edges of the aspect ratio for YouTube. I love the first one that a band really stood behind, "Pale Blue Eyes" for The Kills, even though the transfer isn't great quality. I love all the ones on Ektachrome, especially the Hunx videos, because that venue doesn't exist anymore, and for awhile Ektachrome didn't either.

"In the punk scene there is a storied history of women especially filming or photographing the events. I felt protected by my camera."

What is the cinevinyl record jector?

It's an analog music video machine: a combined super 8mm projector and vinyl record player that plays in sync, housed in one piece.

Where did the idea for the Cinevinyl come from?

When I got the footage back from the first time I shot a band on film I saw the gap that lay between cutting the video in Premiere (I cut all my footage digitally) and posting it on YouTube, but holding the reel of film in my hand and its corresponding song on 7" vinyl. It all dawned on me one night after I went to a party by myself. I was sitting in my parents' freezing cold basement, coming down from medicinal marijuana, and I imagined this device to sync and play together a vinyl record with a super 8 projector. Being that the technologies are so analogous - they each last 3-10 minutes at a time, they were each hugely popularized, DIY formats, and they were created at the same time - I thought this already existed. Google told me that was not quite so. Timing was very lucky. I started working on

it right away and the same month acquired some pieces from Dragan Stojanovic at Black and White Film Factory (which was shutting down that month). I also ended up buying a 16mm projector, super 8 telecine, Bolex, reel to reel recorder, and contact printer from him eventually. I was inspired by the upswing of vinyl and Third Man Records novelties, as well as researching the early cinema machines, which were very odd and experimental.

As someone who records live shows, do you consider yourself an archivist or documentarian at all?

Very much so. In the punk scene there is a storied history of women especially filming or photographing the events. I felt protected by my camera. I always felt that preserving these events on physical film was important. Regardless of the commercial success of the music or of myself, I loved to have gestures, audiences, and all the spontaneity of each of these evenings in my attic. Now some of the bands have broken up, the venues are closing, and I'm thinking of how to move forward. It does mean something to me that I'll always have those images, and I think it means something to the artists to see themselves represented in such a monumental-looking format.

Anything else to add?

I'd really like to film more women, and particularly women of color. Most of my videos are of boy bands. I'm aware of that now and addressing how to contribute in a more intersectional way. I also want to film women's boxing, horse-racing, and food. I'm currently working on a feature film.

I have an origin story about Direct Cinema. Monterey Pop made me into a serious filmmaker - one specific shot - when Otis Redding performs "I've Been Loving You For Too Long" and the light flares into the lens so purely white and expressively. I met D.A. Pennebaker at Hot Docs 2018, and he was so sweetly shocked that I remembered that shot. He shared with me that Robbie Robertson had told him to get rid of the shots because they were technically flawed, and D.A. couldn't do it, and then within a week heard the news of Otis's tragic death, and felt compelled to keep it.

THE
REAL
THING

Julianna Villarosa

Julianna Villarosa is a filmmaker and moving image artist from Texas. Her work addresses human-environment relationships. Select features and screenings include Vimeo Staff Picks, Hong Kong Arts Centre, The Atlantic, Athens International Film + Video Festival, Discovery Channel, the National Park Service, and more. She is a 2019 Tallgrass Artist-in-Residence, Digital Scholarship & Publishing Studio Fellow, and MFA candidate in Film & Video Production at the University of Iowa.

What inspired *The Real Thing*?

When I was living in Atlanta, I worked for Coca-Cola making ads. I had some unsavory experiences there. Then about two weeks after I left that job, that was when the scandal about Chiapas and water privatization broke. I spent a long time feeling guilty about my involvement in that in some capacity, and I wanted to make something that would right a wrong. And that's how *The Real Thing* was born. It was one of my first projects working with film and it was a giant time commitment with regards to learning how to hand develop film or what happens if you soak undeveloped film in Coca-Cola for a few days. It turned out so cool, but there were just so many unknowns going into it. It felt like a science experiment.

Did you use both VHS and film?

It was VHS and film. I had done a lot of VHS work in the past and I loved everything about VHS. My husband and I are actually together because we saw each other's VHS collections. That's always been a really big part of my life, and when I developed the film that I used for *The Real Thing* it was black and white, but it's gone to sepia tone from the Coca-Cola. Color was a really important part of that commercial, because it's multicultural, and everybody's wearing these costumes from their different homes. I know that's really hokey and I wanted people to get the hokiness of it. It's this commercial from a giant company and they're trying to reach as many people as they possibly can. I felt like color was something that I really needed to be in this piece, and that's how VHS came into it.

Did you use Coca-Cola as a developer or use it to distress the film after developing?

Both. I had read of course about caffenol and realized I could sub Coca-Cola for coffee in this case. I ended up making a developer, I call it Coca-Cola-nol.

What other work do you do with VHS?

A few years ago I made this VHS mixed tape with my friend Josh Yates who is also an Iowa graduate. I started it because I felt like short videos were underrecognized by film festivals. I think there is a lot of power to the short video, so I wanted to make something that was a celebration of short videos. We ended up making a super cut of all these video submissions that we got over the course of the year and released it on 30 VHS tapes. I'm really glad to say all 30 are gone. I wasn't really expecting anything from that project but it turned out to be really fun.

What is your process when working with VHS?

For the Real Thing, I unspooled the tape and I dipped my fingers in Coca-Cola and I really lightly touched it, I respooled the tape and then I digitized that and that's how I got these warps in the tape. Even with just touching the tape with your bare fingers, the oils interact with the tape and that creates distortion. I like practical effects, I'm not one whose going to go onto aftereffects and apply a fake VHS filter, so I try to do everything practically.

Do you have a favorite festival, or place that you've screened at?

I just went to Indie grits film festival in Columbia, South Carolina and they're really cool. They treat filmmakers really well. And they are located in the South. Their programing a lot of more progressive and experimental and that's really cool to see.

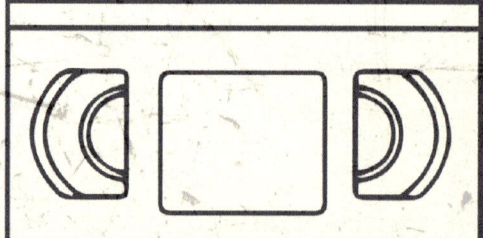

Coca-Colanol Recipe:

2 gallons Coca-Cola Classic (roughly 4 2-liters)
400 grams washing soda
80 grams vitamin c powder

@ 82 degrees F
15-16 minutes of (bucket) processing

As a note: I've tried developing at room
temperature, but the developing time goes way, way
up (around 1 hour of agitating + resting).

I collaborated with German filmmaker Dagie Brundert
on this Coca-Colanol recipe. She mainly develops
with a lomo tank, so it took some trial and error
to adapt this to bucket processing. She has a ton
of resources for developing with other organic
materials. **-Julianna Villarosa**

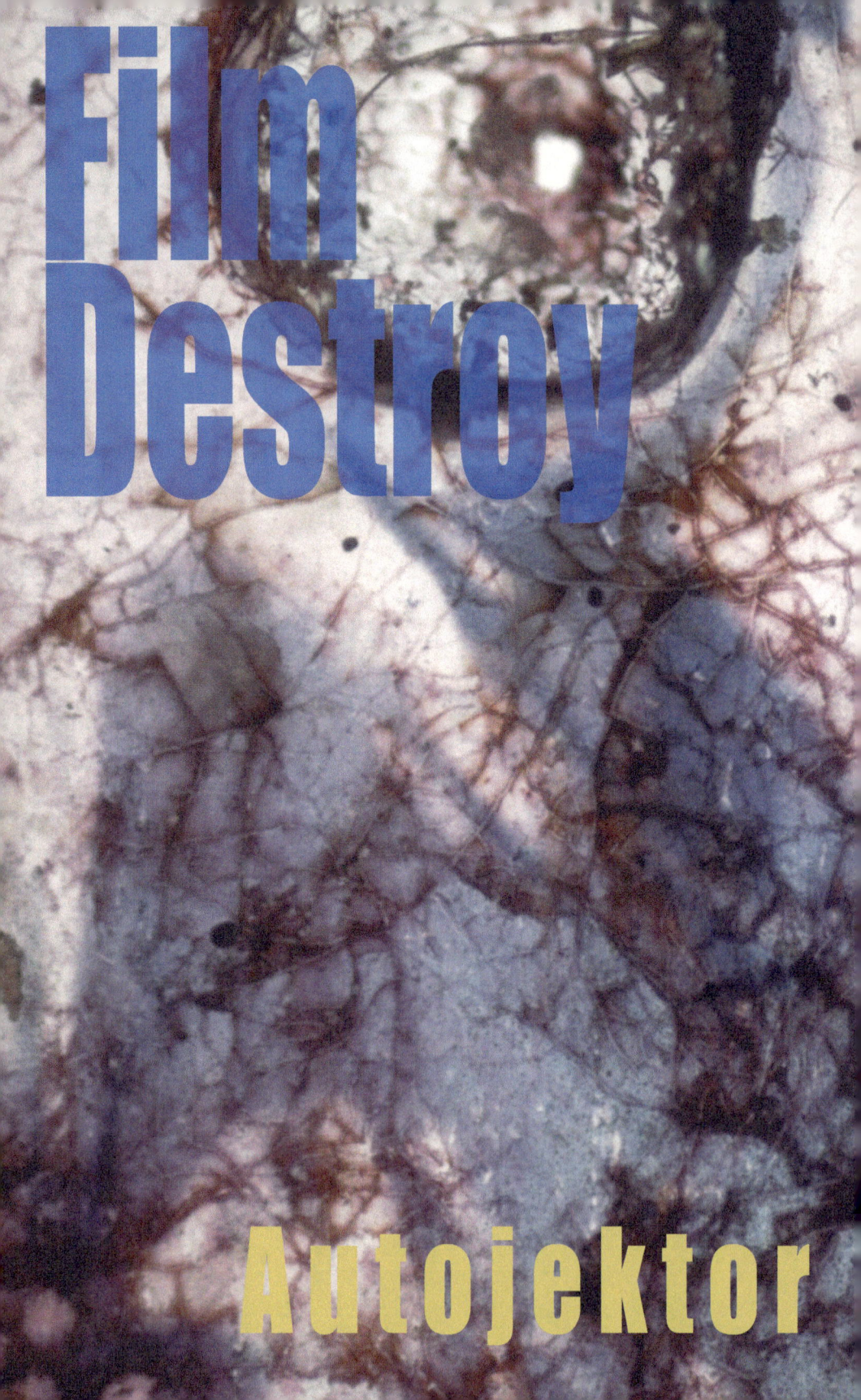

Film Destroy

Autojektor

Autojektor is a cameraless filmmaker based in Southeast London who destroys home movies using bleach and a soldering iron to distress super 8mm film, creating unique shorts and music videos.

How would you describe your process?

It all starts with salvaging home movies; going through reels upon reels of footage and cutting them down into a short series of moments. It's the destruction of these moments that creates the film. I tend to push towards more horror elements in my narratives; I will experiment with ideas of disfiguration, death and erasure, so the techniques I use have to mimic that violence. Whether I burn, rot or bleed on the film, its this process applied to that chain of moments that governs the meaning of each piece.

Super 8mm is so small! In the music video for Closet Witch's song Funeral Regrets, how are you burning such a tiny portion of the film with such precision?

It's a lot of care and a lot of patience. I have a DIY light-box with a magnifying glass duct taped to it and a very small soldering iron.

Super 8mm often evokes feelings of nostalgia. How are you using the medium to re-frame nostalgia and home movies?

The cool thing about super 8 is that we have this symbolic relationship with it, even people who were not necessarily around to experience it can have the same emotional attachment, it's the rose-tinted glasses of film formats. Since starting with 8mm I have been interested in breaking those glasses and creating these short horror vignettes that highlight the fear of loss that exists behind those warm feelings of nostalgia.

What's been your favorite piece you've worked on so far?

They've all had their ups and downs, most of the processes can get quite painful. I've had a couple of films where the primary material has been my own blood and the process behind "Ageless Museums of Rotting Animals" involved burying the footage in meat and allowing it to rot, so reclaiming that wasn't exactly a good time. They've all been worth it though.

What's next for you?

Transgenderism and the occult.

In the spirit of sharing film recipes, do you have a recipe or technique you could share?

Probably the most versatile tool I've worked with is bleach. It eats into the emulsion in layers, allowing you to isolate particular colors or even delete the image entirely. It can leave you with some unearthly neon blues and greens that bleed into the rest of the frame in a beautifully eerie way.

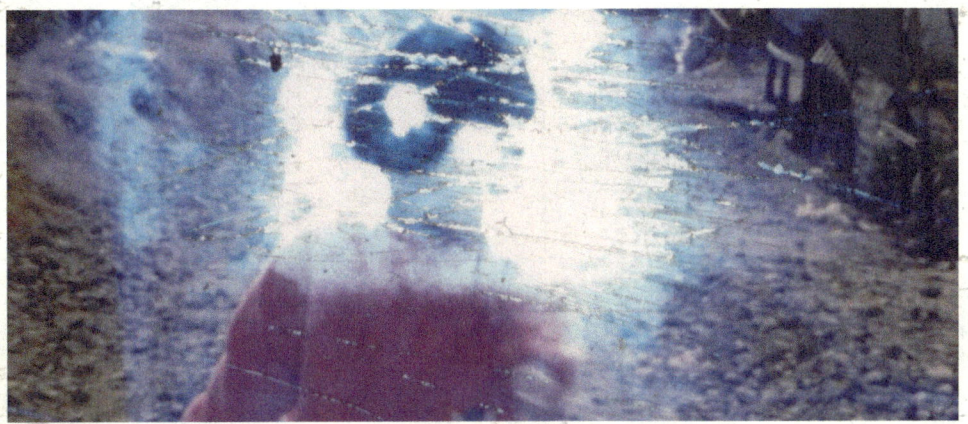

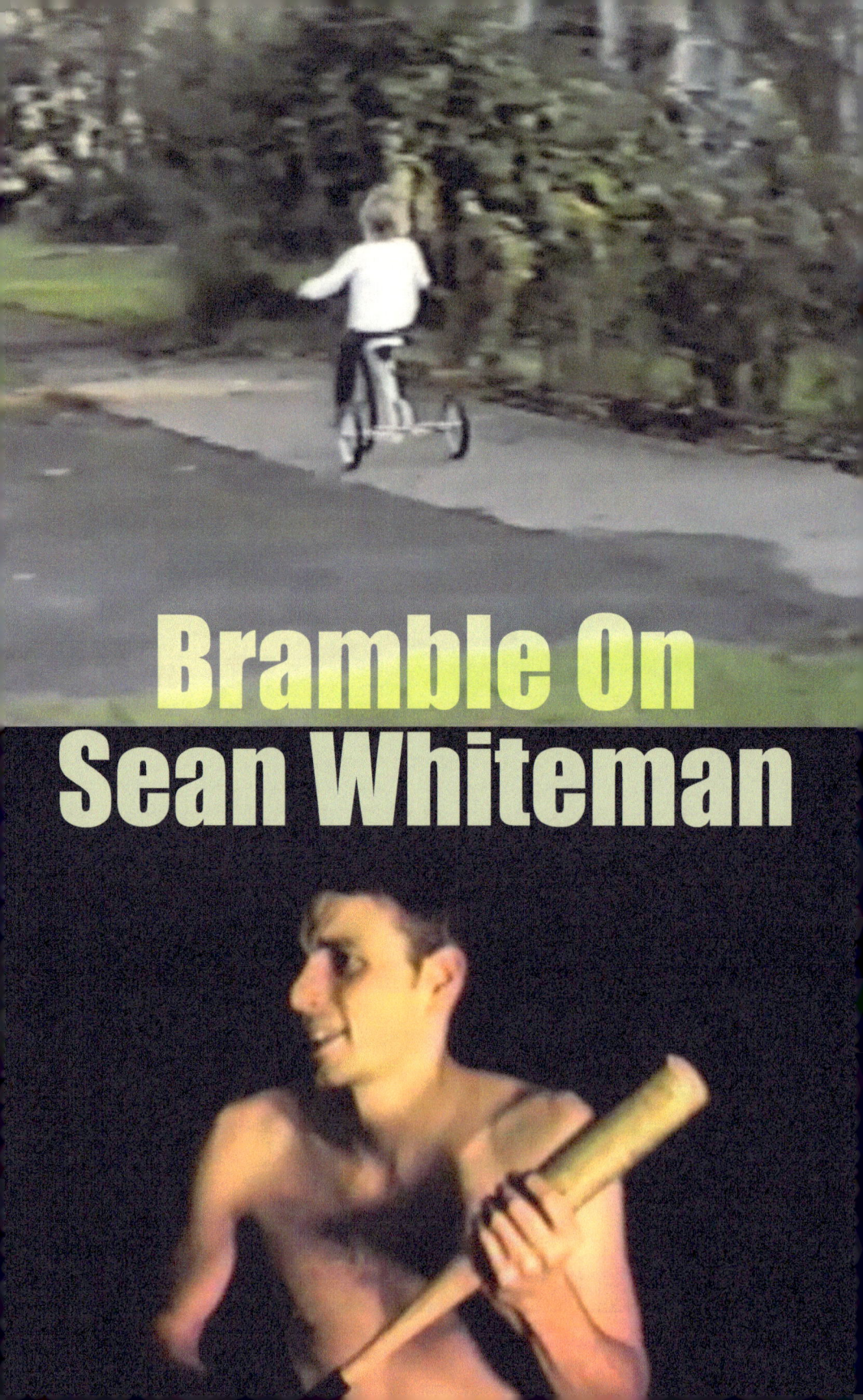

Bramble On
Sean Whiteman

"Because we don't know when we will die, we get to think of life an inexhaustible well."

Halfway through Sean Whiteman's VHS short *Bramble On* we hear these words by author Paul Bowles from the Bernardo Bertolucci's 1990 adaptation of *The Sheltering Sky*. It is this bit of found footage that shifts the tone of the short from one of tongue and cheek horror to a meditation on mortality and childhood as Sean works together a live action narrative with stop-motion animations of vines coupled with found home VHS video.

Sean is a filmmaker based in Portland, Oregon where he works at the Hollywood Theater–a historic non-profit movie theater that's been around since 1926 and still shows film. "I gravitated to the Hollywood Theater for analog reasons," Sean said. "When everybody went digital, they were one of the last places in Portland to hold firm."

Sean has always felt drawn to film and shoots 35mm still photography, though when shooting moving image, he typically opts for digital instead of celluloid due to the high cost. VHS, on the other hand, was more accessible. "There was a period in Portland where everyone was just giving away their VHS tapes. I'd be walking down the street and there's just free piles everywhere of tapes." As a result, Sean's basement became a shrine to video store nostalgia as he collected tapes over the years. For Sean, it's the tangibility of going to a video store that you can't quite get scrolling through Netflix. "I'm just drawn to those sort of experiences of discovering a film or being wowed by some quality that you just can't quite pin down."

Bramble On came to be when Sean stumbled upon a VHS camcorder that a former housemate left in the basement. It didn't quite work, but after a 20-minute YouTube tutorial, he was able to cobble it together with rubber bands and embraces any technical errors the old camcorder creates. "If I move it, it will glitch out. The result is a beautiful technical flourish that I could rely on." In this way, Sean used practical effects for video. "If I knew that I wanted to add a VHS static transition I would do a hard left pan as opposed to a smooth one."

Sean used music by Ryuichi Sakamoto for *Bramble On* as part of an international film competition where the composer called on filmmakers to use music from his album Async to create cinematics works. It was his music that inspired a shift from campy tale of a man investigating the creature in his blackberry brambles to introspective melancholia. "That disposition of being funny and sad is the most fascinating goal in cinema for me. It just shows the dynamic range of humanity."

We watch as the main character, baseball bat in hand, sits in a lawn chair waiting for the creature in the bushes to emerge. We see vines take over his body, fog emerge, and then we're in a montage of home videos that acts as an extended epilogue to the bramble monster's story. We're no longer in the bushes. We're no longer in Portland. We're in the metaphysical space of nostalgia. In every choice he makes, whether it be medium or story, Sean leans into this nostalgia and deep emotional catharsis in *Bramble On*. "Usually the process is an arduous technical and exhausting marathon of productivity," Sean said. "Rarely is it an emotional marathon where you're reliving a good chunk of your life." Like the process itself, watching *Bramble On* is an emotional trip, as it calls into question the fleeting nature of a seemingly inexhaustible well–this time in the form of blackberry brambles.

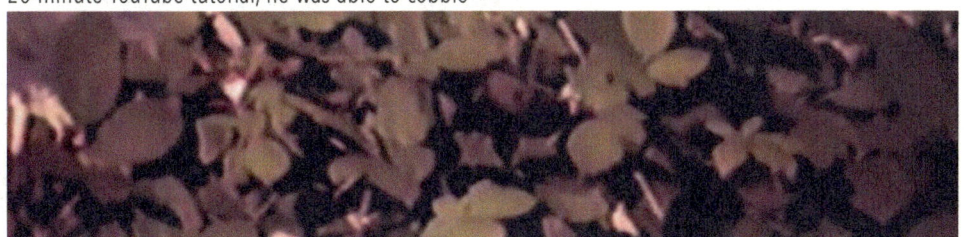

Bio
lumin
escent
Filmmaking

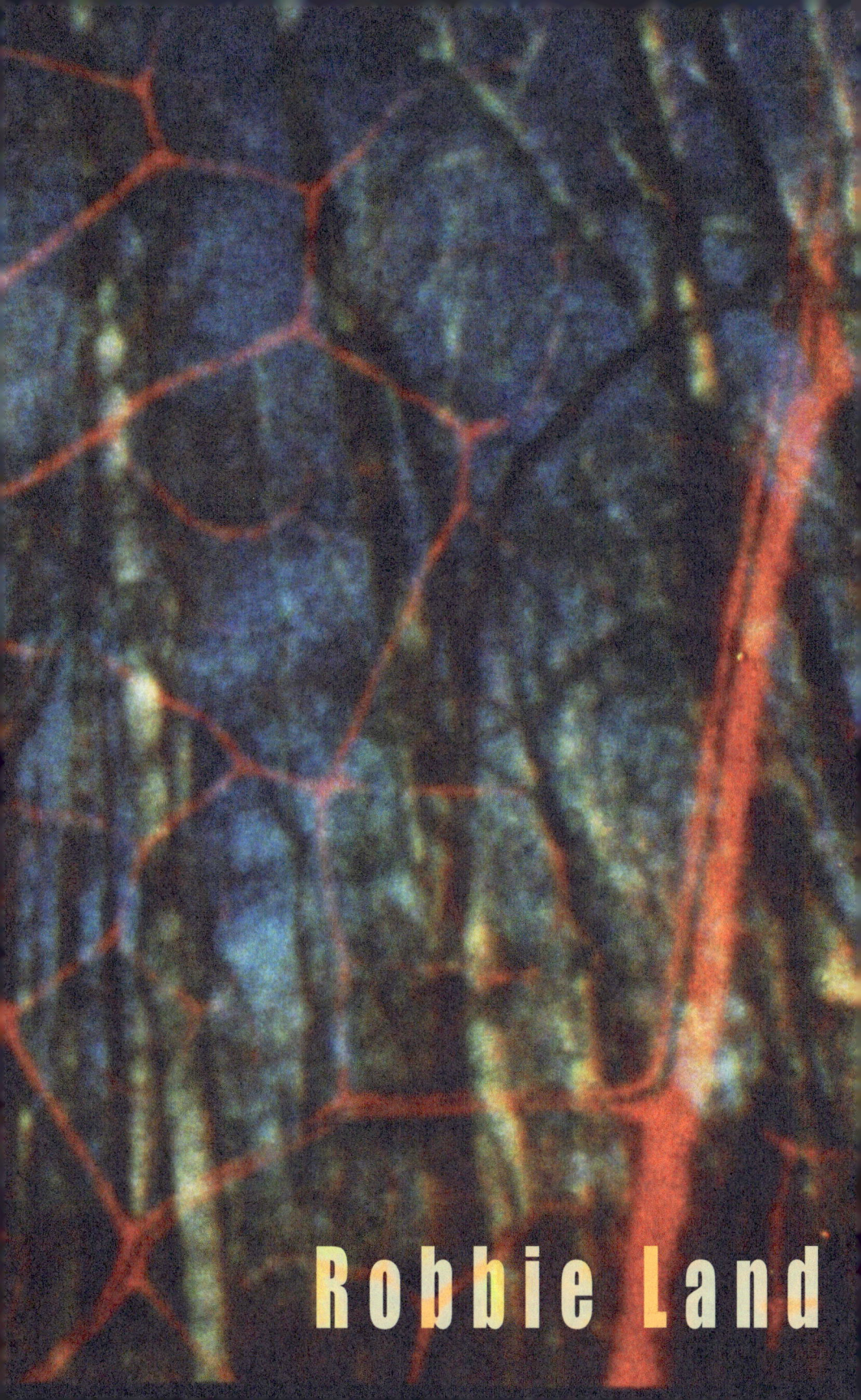

Robbie Land

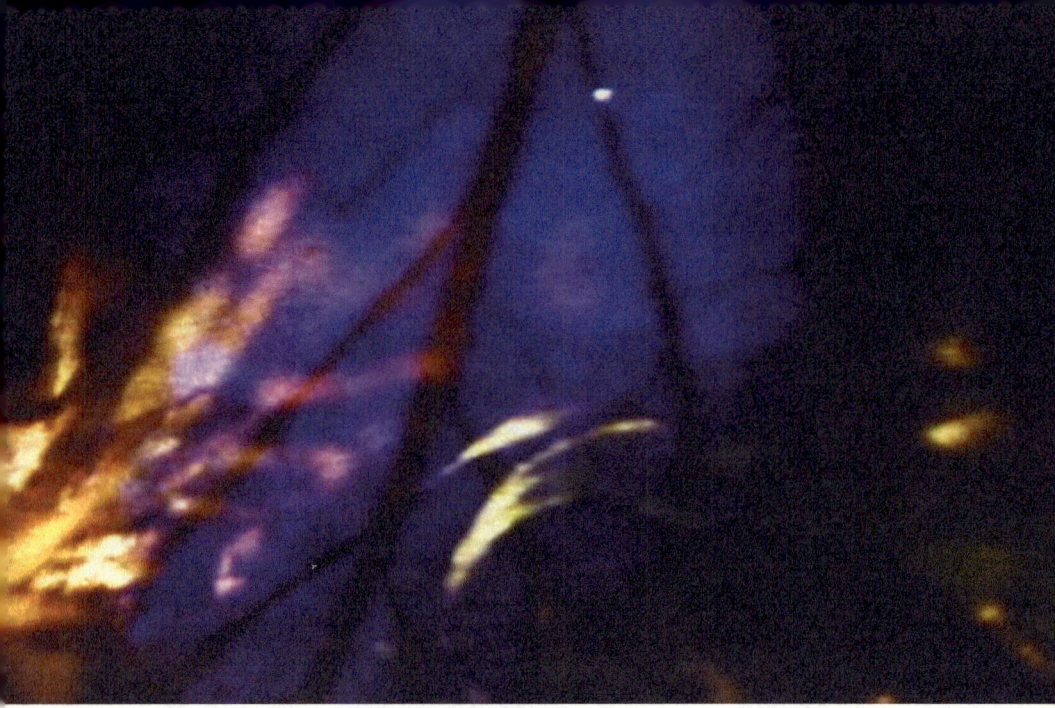

Robbie Land is a visual artist who works mostly with 8mm, 16mm and 35mm celluloid. He is also a lecturer of film production at Georgia State University in Atlanta, Georgia. In his 2006 film Betty Creek he too plants from Betty Creek, Georgia and applied them directly to celluloid in order to create a projected sense of the Appalachian Betty Creek environment. In his 2012 film Matters of Bioluminescence, he used fireflies to directly affect raw 16mm film stock. Building off of themes of nature, location, and direct application of natural material, he is currently working on Grant Park Photosynthesis--a piece about the Grant Park neighborhood in Atlanta that illustrates the landscape and the park's history through this photosynthesis process.

In all three films (*Matters of Bioluminescence, Betty Creek, & Grant Park Photosynthesis*), you're working directly with film and nature. What inspires you to work with nature in this way?
Well, to put it simply, I enjoy the natural sciences and therefore drawn to use subjects and locations in North America to generate a personal perspective, a poetic science to the films I am creating.

How do you typically screen your films?
Usually screen my film work in 16mm with optical sound at various venues and film festivals. I also exhibit this work in installations using film-loopers on continuous loop.

In *Matters of Bioluminescence*, are you placing fireflies in direct contact with raw film stocks? How does the contact between fireflies and celluloid change the fabric of the film?
Yes, in that film, I captured several fireflies, approximately seven and in complete darkness, placed them in a large glass aquarium-like container with plants and unspooled rolls of raw, unexposed light sensitive 16mm film stock. The fireflies did their work over night and the next morning I removed the little bugs from the darkroom and returned them to their environment and processed and printed the film - surprisingly got images. The first portion of the film you'll see a time-exposed sequence of the the fireflies in action, which was filmed with Bolex and time-lapse motor. The film then cuts to the fireflies camera-less resulting images. I had no idea if I would obtain an image from this overnight experiment, the bugs provided. The glowing foxfire mushrooms section of the film was created in a similar manner.

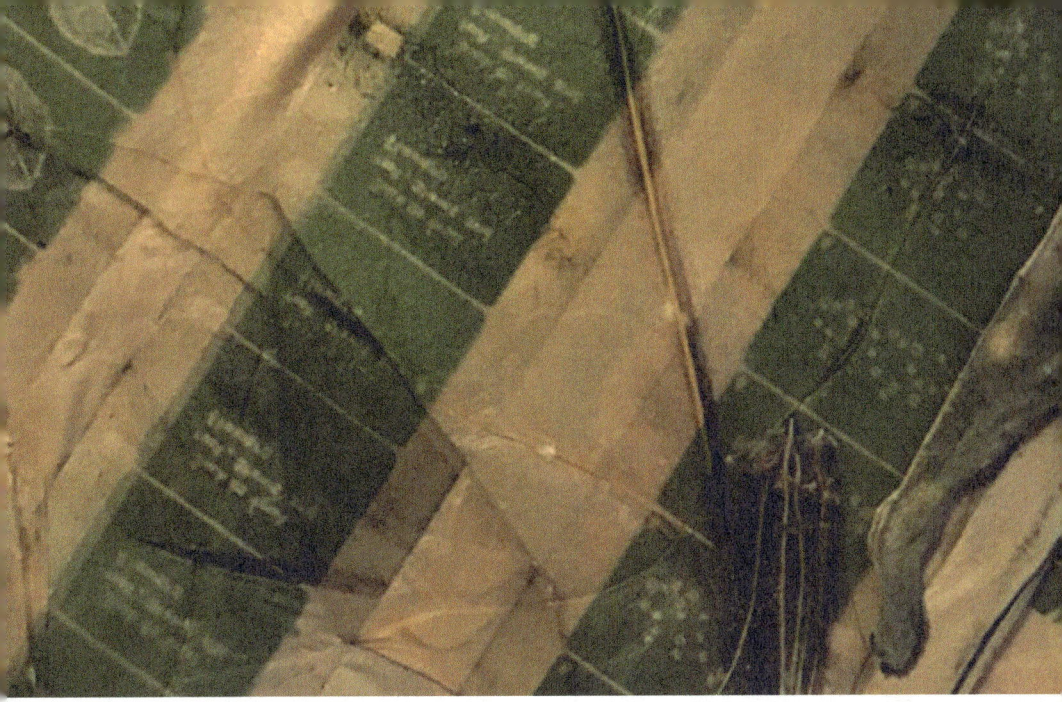

What methods are you using to apply elements from nature to your films?

I utilize various methods to achieve the so-called desired result. Mostly using the direct application or direct animation process. This is a more tactile procedure where I appreciate the hands-on process of working with organic material creating specific images on film stock. In order to obtain that desired result, I experiment with many methods and tools, conventional or unconventional to achieve the perspective I feel properly represents the view I hope to achieve for each subject.

Both Betty Creek and Grant Park Photosynthesis are about specific locations in Georgia. Why are these places special to you?

The locations are special to me, which is obviously why I chose them, but the concept and procedure to create the film work focusing any space or location is more and documenting it in the cinematic direct application form is exciting. Therefore, I like the idea or result of illustrating anything using this cinematic application to expose any place.

What advice would you give to up and coming camera-less analog filmmakers?

To camera-less analog filmmakers, be destructive, try things, explore beyond your comfort. Do not hesitate, try things whether you think it will work or not.

What's next for you?

Currently working on a film I shot in Newfoundland Canada while on a residency. This film focuses on the people and their fishing villages on that island the locals call a rock. I used Regular-8mm film to capture the raw crudeness of this beautiful location and its dwellers. I'm now in the process of enlarging the 8mm images using JK optical printer to 16mm negative.

In addition, I am developing a second chapter to the Grant Park Photosynthesis film. In this next chapter, I am using various techniques in order to produce a more detailed perspective of this specific location. These methods include rotoscoping, re-photography, optical printing and the photosynthesis contact printing process. This process involves shooting high-contrast 16mm film in the Grant Park location, collecting leaves from that location, placing the processed film over the leaves (contact printing) and exposing to sunlight for one to two days, if we have sun. The exposure varies obviously according to sunlight and time of year. In addition to the footage I shoot in the park, I am illustrating and rotoscoping images from historic and current image sequences of the Grant Park area.

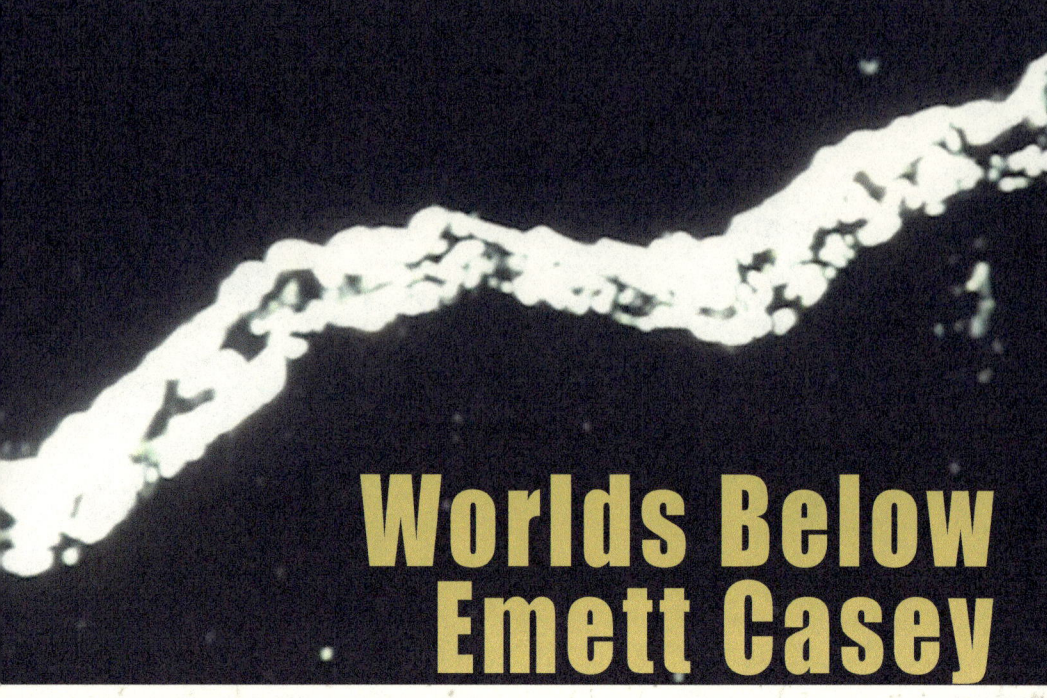

Worlds Below
Emett Casey

Emett Casey is a Los Angeles based filmmaker. His work has been shown at theaters, festivals, galleries and micro cinemas around the U.S. and abroad. Working in both short form and features, his work ranges between abstract and poetic narrative.

What inspired Worlds Below?

World's Below came about through the Mike Kelley Foundations' Artist Grant, which was given to the Co-op Members of Echo Park Film Center. There are about twenty of us in the co-op who run the Film Center, and we all wanted to make short pieces about Los Angeles.

Unlike the stereotype, I tend to walk a lot around L.A. And one thing you notice when you walk around L.A. is that the sidewalks are in very, very rough shape. A lot of this is due to the trees that line the sidewalk. The City designers have planted trees with buttress root system, which push up into the sidewalks, cracking and disrupting them. And, where there aren't trees with such root systems, the trees roots are abnormally high because the City sucks out the ground water, forcing the root structure to come to the surface to get surface water. I was noticing the beautiful roots breaking through the concrete, but also the similarity is shape to the sidewalk cracks. There seemed a kind of rhyme and rhythm there. It was a part of Los Angeles literally below our noses, and I thought I'd make a film about it.

What was your process making Worlds Below?

I used a Bolex on a Bolex Titler for most of the photography. I'd go out with a roll or two -

sometimes color, sometimes B&W - and do eight to twelve single frame shots of the cracks that I liked as I walked along Sunset Blvd. in Echo Park. Occasionally I shot with actual motion. There are a few shots where I tilted the Titler to sort of rock into the frame. I used lenses with close focus less than a foot, or at times extension tubes or a macro slider to get very close. When I got the film back there was something about it that reminded me of geographical survey photography - especially some high contrast B&W stuff. It looked both macro and micro, at times like large landscapes. I really liked that element to it.

Next I did very rough edits of what I thought would go well together - basically organizing the footage onto rolls. Then there was several months on a JK Optical Printer. I shot and reshot and reshot the reshoots with different color filters and bipacks. I added a few frames of hand painted film bipacked in at one point, too. Generally speaking, I worked in what I thought of as movements. Sometimes I'd be in the middle of shooting something on the JK and I'd realize what I was working on actually belonged earlier or later because of texture or rhythm or whatever. So I'd shoot it anyway and then make notes to put it into the earlier stuff.

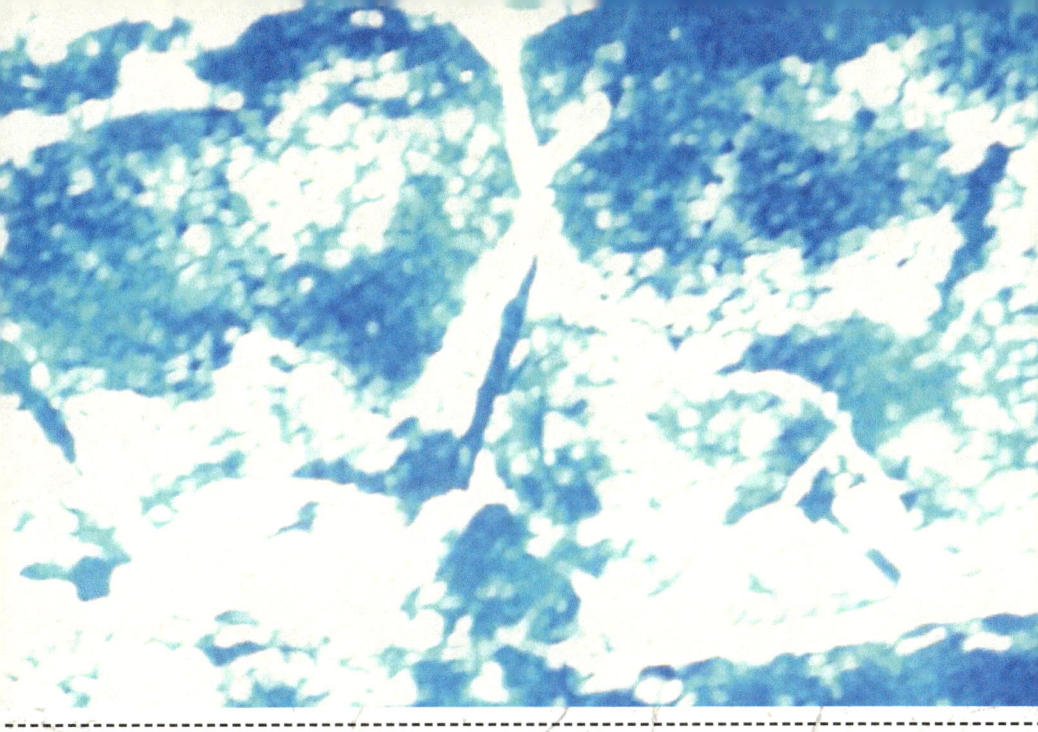

Because I worked on the JK, rephotographing the edits, I had only about 15 edits to make when it came to the negative cutting. So I decided to cut the negative myself, something I'd never done before. Luckily, my friend Andrew Kim was kind enough to show me some pointers. I designed most of the edits to be on frames of black, so I was able to do an A-Roll only negative edit. Then I got a print made at the lab. And there you have it.

Tell us a bit about Echo Park Film Center and the work you do with them.

Echo Park Film Center has been in Los Angeles for coming on 18 years. It is a non-profit media arts center, which focuses on providing equal and affordable community access to film and video. It is run by a co-op of 20 or so of us, who help keep the space alive. We serve as a micro cinema, a library and equipment retail space, offer free and nominal cost education programs, an eco-friendly mobile film school which goes around LA teaching and doing screenings, and also do local and international artist residencies. It is a really lively and lovely community, offering a beautiful alternative to the Hollywood narrative of film and video. I first ran some screenings there back in 2008, and then about four or five years ago became part of the co-op.

What's been your favorite work you've shot on film?

My favorite work I've shot on film, is probably the rolls that didn't turn out. They live in this beautiful what-could-it-have-been world. There was specifically a large parade I filmed once on Kodachrome that turned out completely blank. It was 300 feet of a jubilee procession that lead to an execution on a misty morning. The beheading happened right as the mist cleared and these God-rays shot down. I think about it every now and then - a kind of Pasolini type thing in Kodachrome.

Favorite place to screen analog works?

Echo Park Film Center. The love and the family is there.

Do you have a recipe you can share?

For Worlds Below I used Sound Track stock for the high contrast shots. I would rephotograph on the JK a piece of color film in this ultra high con, but over-expose it by 3/4 a stop. Then cross process it so I had a positive, dry it, bring it back and bipack it with the color image. Then rephotograph the bipack. The resulting black in the shadows and contrast gives a very specific look to everything. There's also sometimes a little ghostly type effect if they don't line up perfectly.

Anything else we should know?

Most of my stuff is available online at emettcasey. com, but most of the analog stuff I do I prefer to show on film. So much of the rhythm and textures get lost in the digital world.

Developing

film

with

Coffee

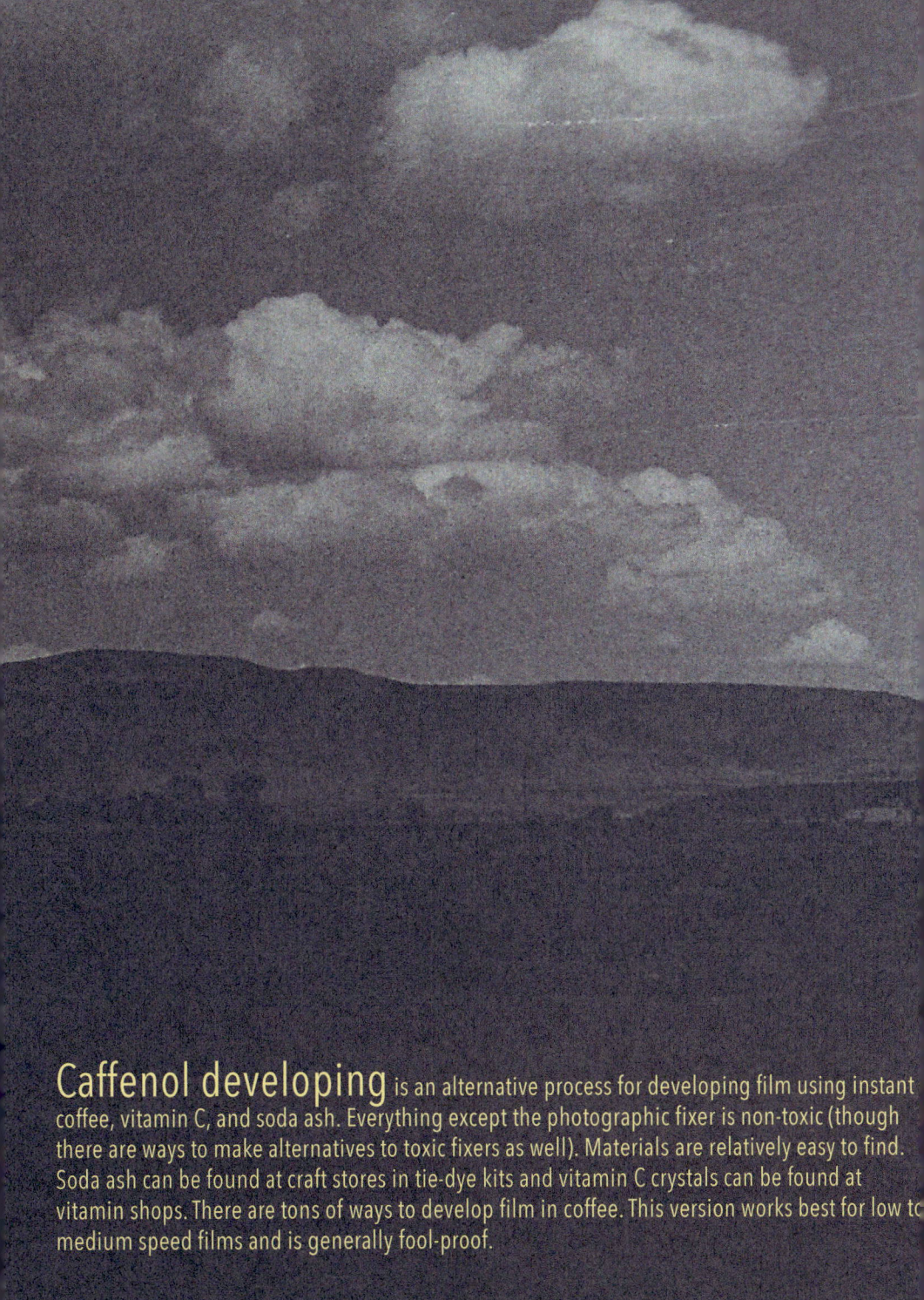

Caffenol developing is an alternative process for developing film using instant coffee, vitamin C, and soda ash. Everything except the photographic fixer is non-toxic (though there are ways to make alternatives to toxic fixers as well). Materials are relatively easy to find. Soda ash can be found at craft stores in tie-dye kits and vitamin C crystals can be found at vitamin shops. There are tons of ways to develop film in coffee. This version works best for low to medium speed films and is generally fool-proof.

Ingredients

*12 oz Room temperature water

*25g Instant coffee

*3g Vitamin C crystals

*18g Water-free washing soda (AKA soda ash)

*12oz photographic fixer

Make the developer

-Mix instant coffee into 6oz of water and stir until crystals are dissolved
-Add vitamin C to coffee mixture and stir
-In a separate bowl, mix washing soda into remaining 6oz of water
-Combine mixtures

Develop

-Pour mixture into tank. Set timer for 9:00 minutes
-For the first minute agitate constantly
-Repeat agitation once ever minute
-Pour out developer when timer stops

Rinse

-Pour room temp water into tank, agitate and pour out
-Repeat until water runs clear

Fix

-Pour fixer into tank and set timer for 5 minutes
-Agitate once every minute
-Pour leftover fix back to be reused when timer is done.

Materials

*Scale

*Mixing bowls, tupperware etc.

*Developing tank

*Optional: thermometer, funnel, drying rack

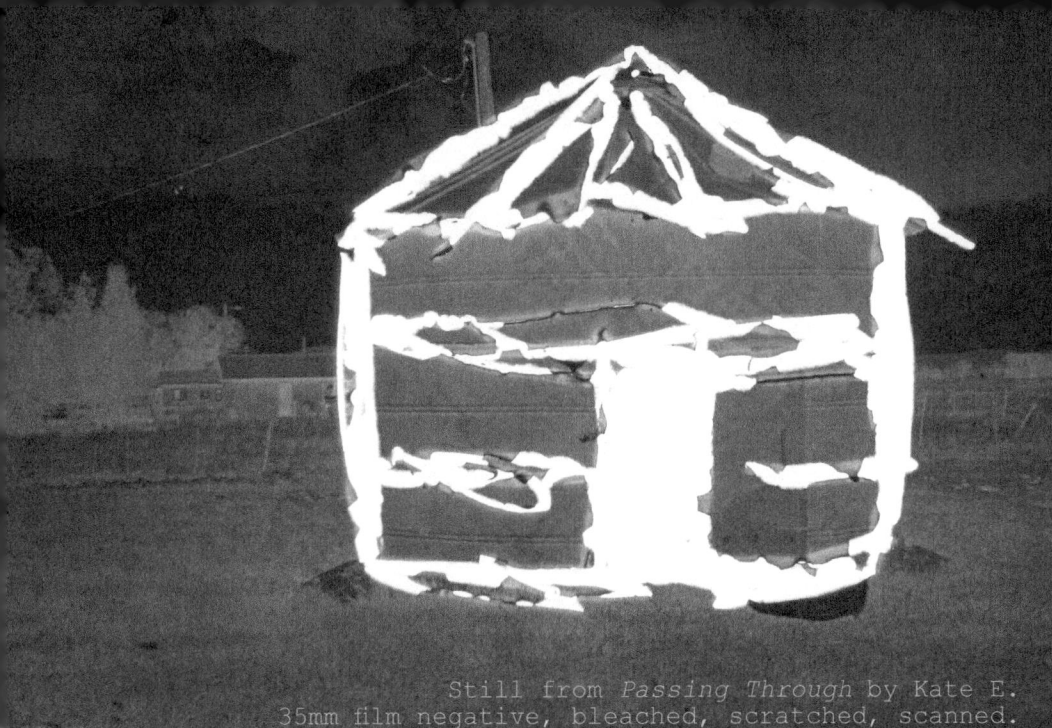

Still from *Passing Through* by Kate E.
35mm film negative, bleached, scratched, scanned.

Things you can do with your brand new Caffenol negatives

Paint them with India ink.

Bleach and scratch them.

Challenge your need to be perfect.

Shoot, develop, and scan them all in the same day.

Cover them in stickers.

Fold it up accordion style and dunk it in bleach.

Admire them as is and leave them be.

Pas De Deux

Paul DeSilva is a filmmaker from Portland, Oregon currently residing in Brooklyn, NY. When he's not making short films, music videos, or working on other indie shorts, he works as a freelance animator, motion designer. Currently, he's at Teen Vogue where he handles all the Motion Design for their Snapchat channel. His film Pas De Deux is a short film about love and loss told in a dreamy world crafted through hand-processed 16mm film.

Where did the idea of Pas de Deux come from? Any relation to the Norman McLaren film of the same name?

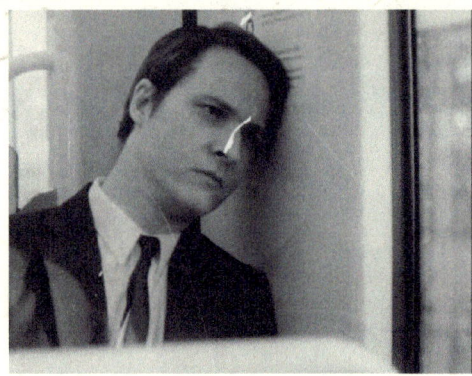

In 2007, I met a gal in film school who I became pretty enamored with. A year after graduation, we were married and living in Vancouver, Canada. I'd landed my first job at a local VFX company and she was grinding it out as a PA on a few different shows. The hours were long for both of us but we were young and just happy to be building up our demo reels. The unfortunate side-effect was that she would often have to be on set by 6am, getting home at some point in the evening and going to bed early to meet the next day's 6am call time. I was mon-fri, starting work at 10am, often going until 10pm or later as we approached deadlines. When she left for work, I was asleep, and when I got home from work, so was she. We slowly became to each other only the things we left behind. I watched a bookmark travel down a book day by day without ever seeing it open. She watched the leftovers from crafty she'd put in the fridge disappear every night. This carried on for about a year or so before our relationship succumbed to the

strain of it and we parted ways.

Years later, I was kicking around an idea of two people who got trapped in the same body and had to take turns living out their days. I figured the toughest part would be that they could never directly see each other or communicate. Once I'd made the connection from that to my failed marriage, I knew it was what I wanted to pursue as the concept for my next film and Pas de Deux is what came out of that.

As for the name, I had actually seen this piece by Daniel Wurtzel bearing the same name that featured two silks surrounded by an array of fans forcing them to dance around each other. A little research taught me that a Pas de Deux was a style of ballet written for two, usually a man and woman, and occasionally requiring them to make the same exact movements, so I thought the name would be a good fit. Of course, that also led me to McLaren's film which I instantly fell in love with. I have these 3 sequences in my film that are meant to be sort of dream spaces where the two people can meet in the time between switching from one to the other. I decided to go for a really high contrast look in a black void as a small nod to McLaren's film.

What film stock did you shoot on and how was it processed?

From the start, I'd decided I wanted not only to shoot on film, but to develop it by hand and figure out some way to digitize it myself as well. Over the years, I had shot plenty of 35mm still photography but since this was my first foray into motion picture film, I didn't feel quite ready to go experimenting with stocks and processes; I would be happy just to see an image emerge on the film at all! I had access to a few stocks but in the end, I went with Kodak Double-X 7222 because it seemed like it was low contrast enough to give me latitude to fix any metering mistakes I knew I would likely make. I bought the recommended Kodak developer and fixer (D-76) and tried to follow the instructions to my best ability so my recipe was the standard Developer 7 minutes, Stop Bath 1 minute, Fixer 10 minutes. Unfortunately, I did this in my very unventilated bathroom and got pretty sick for about 3 days after doing all the developing, with a cough that persisted for the next month or so. I was able to develop the 12x 100' rolls I'd shot over 3 nights. Drying the film actually proved to be the most difficult because I thought I'd be able to sort of coil it on the floor but that definitely didn't work. At the time, I was living on the 3rd floor of an apartment building so I hung the film off my balcony and it would hover a few feet off the sidewalk and dried in the wind pretty quickly.

Once this was done, I had to figure out a way to digitize it. I messed around with a few different methods before settling on using a DSLR with a projection lens I had scavenged from an old 16mm projector taped backward onto the camera lens. A friend who had an optical printer let me use it so I was able to mount the camera to that and get the optics lined up just so to take a fairly full frame macro image of each 16mm frame as a 4k RAW CR2 file. Then I sat in that room for 8 hours a day over the course of a few days just clicking advance on the optical printer, then snapping a photo, advance on the optical printer, snap a photo, rinse, repeat about 40,000 times until I had an image sequence of all the footage I'd shot. From there I went to digital editing. I would not recommend that anybody tries this at home.

What films and Filmmakers inspire you?
For me, the 70's will always be the renaissance of film and I tend to gravitate towards those Filmmakers that embody that surrealist, psychotic quality like Kenneth Anger, Jodorowsky, John Waters, Cassevetes. On the other hand, I also love those more deliberate, technical Filmmakers like Tarkovsky and Kubrik who approach similarly bizarre subject matter from the opposing angle. I've always struggled with what sort of filmmaker I want to be, an emotional experimenter or a calculating fabricator, so I think I bounce back in forth in my influences and in my work.

A few of your films deal with dream space and pull from your own dreams. Can you talk a bit about that?
I've always thought that dreams and films have an important commonality in that they both portray distorted versions of reality. In narrative film, we always talk about not trying to break the suspension of disbelief, but that's something that happens to you automatically when you dream. You get taken on this weird journey that you can't really control and it feels like reality but can be completely absurd upon waking examination. Films are similar, or are perhaps the closest you can get to being able to show someone a dream you had.

What's been your favorite festival or venue to screen your work?
When I finished my first film, 'A Spark at Darkest Night', I was very fortunate to get to premiere it at the Toronto International Film Festival. Working on the film over the course of the prior year in my humble living room and only ever seeing it on a laptop screen, I truly had no preconceptions that it would ever be exhibited on a screen larger than a foot wide. Getting to see it projected enormously in a packed theater running alongside a handful of incredibly crafted shorts from around the world was absolutely incredible. I went for the entire duration of the festival and, because I had an all access pass, watched about 4 features per day for a week. It was a once in a lifetime experience (unless I can somehow trick another festival into thinking my films are any good).

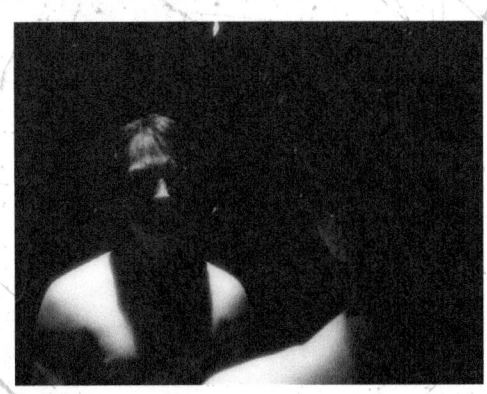

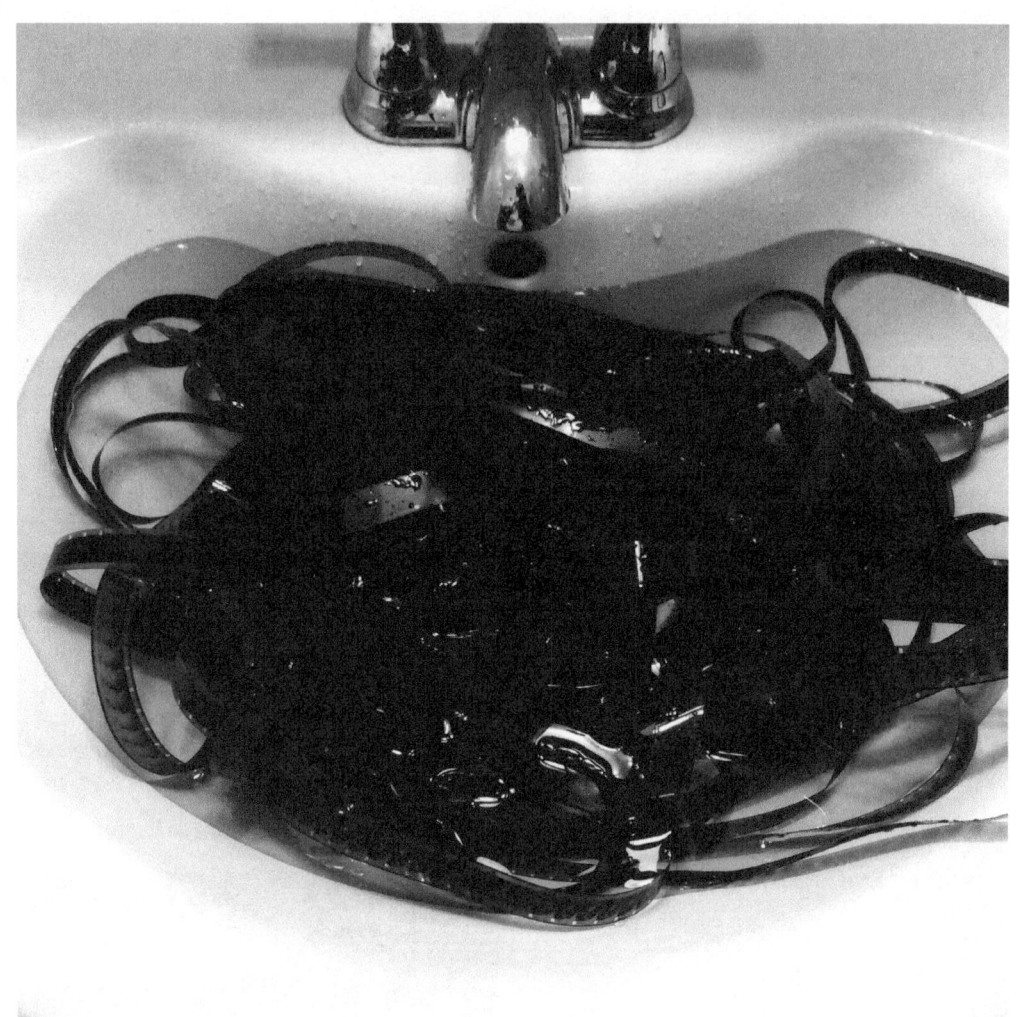

photo by Paul DeSilva

L.O.V.E.S.O.N.G.

by Tetsuya Maruyama
Rio de Janeiro, Brazil

"Everytime a projector cries, a love song is sculpted in the magnetic field"

This film is consisted simply of transparent super 8 film and magnetic audio cassette tape applied on the other side of perforation area for the duration that one roll can hold. The reason why I started this practice is not solely a question of aesthetics, but rather an economic/infrastructural necessity. In South America, generally speaking, infrastructure around analog filmmaking is very weak compared to the countries in the northern hemisphere. If you have financial resources, you could try importing products from outside the country, but the postal system here is very complicated. They get lost on the way or you end up paying ridiculous amounts of import taxes. Here in Brazil, there are some small artist-run practices, mainly in São Paulo and Rio de Janeiro, but it is impossible to acquire new Kodak cartridges. The only place in South America where you can find an authorized Kodak importer is in Buenos Aires.

All these things considered, it was not easy to find transparent super 8 film. The film used on this project was found in a flea market in a square called Praça 15, in downtown Rio de Janeiro. On the case, the title says, "Wedding Monique and Isaac March 27th 1980, Rio de Janeiro." I could tell by the footage that it was a wealthy family since the film had a soundtrack and titles at the beginning and the end. The wedding was held in a synagogue and the film was consisted of two parts, a reception at home and ceremony in a civil office. Considering the historical value of the film, it was a hard decision to erase the images by household bleach to obtain a transparent film. After bleaching, there was still another question: applying the tape on film. I knew by principle the mechanism of reading sonic information on tape. I have used cassette tape for the last 20 years for recording banal sounds in life. However, I have never done a montage of cassette tape by applying to another medium. Therefore, I had to execute various experiments with different types of glues; regular white glue for paper, Styrofoam glue, super glue, glue for photography, glue without toxic materials, etc. After a couple weeks of testing all these glues, I found out that applying an amount of a regular multipurpose glue without solvent, just enough to cover the area of tape, works the best. The first attempt failed badly with glue falling inside the projector gate and corridor, and ended up jamming most of the film. After the second or the third attempt, even though the film warped a little bit because of the glue, there was no problem of passing a film through the projector. And the sound!!!! It must be highlighted that the tape used for this film was completely new, which means, theoretically no sound recorded. It is still a wonder how it worked (producing sound), and I must continue on this experiment by modifying size, texture, type of glue, fermentation on tape itself, or even recording sound first and applying on film(or flip this process). The possibility is infinite and I am very happy that it worked.

Revém Natura

Super 8mm Experience by Ж

Ж is a film-designer, educator and programmer. His films, video installations and texts have been exhibited in festivals, galleries and museums including San Francisco Museum of Modern Art, Centre de Cultura Contemporània de Barcelona and Museo San Telmo in San Sebastián, Spain. As an educator he has coordinated the audiovisual formation program *Fazer o Mundo Fazendo Video* and the educational action *SSS_South Small Sister*. His piece *Revém Natura* is a filmic experience that is part of an environmental / ambient program called CI.NE- Natural Expanded Cinema. It addresses and responds to the current state of toxic environmental and political circumstances and screened as part of a public art exhibit called MAPA.

How did you get into making films?

I first became interested in working with moving image in 2008 when I realized that film, media, and thought are time based. Simultaneously, there was an interest in investigating the sensual aspect of thought within the film medium. As we know, thought, ideas, immaterial cultures aren't individuals' constructions or creations. This starting point enabled a reflection about subjectivities that cross the subject center or oriented perspective. This kind of existence goes across and beyond oneself. This subjectivity emerges as a flux through the "inside" and "outside". The Klein bottle could be a good example for that form of existence. I've worked with films, installations, public art, film programs, counter-spaces, texts and books publishing in order to establish this relationship--to stabilize those intensive forces into tangible, readable, danceable, temporary and intensive structures.

What inspired Revém Natura?

Revém Natura took the form of an outdoor film installation, created with two super 8mm film projectors, two west oriented prepared screens, and the privileged presence of the pacific ocean. For this project it was important to synchronize and be oriented by the sunset. Because of the peculiar light, the atmosphere created, the common contemplation moment, and the direct light needed to illuminate the back of the screens or order to generate shadows with texts and a fixed image, the space where the work exhibited influenced a lot of its production. The first idea was that it will happen only once. It was a situated film in that it was made possible by those specific time-space conditions. It goes beyond site specific. The work was made in the context of the research for my thesis called CI NE. Cine Natural Expandido (Natural Expanded Cinema in English)

What is MAPA?

MAPA was a public art program held in Mazunte y Mermejita - Oaxaca, Mexico in 2013 with myself and the filmmaker Carla Lombardo. It emerged from a desire to thank people's village for their intense, strong, and careful reception of us. It was also an exhibition of the work we developed in 2012 while we were living there. The program occurred along 15 days was this public art time suspension. Our aim was to suggest a duration more than an event. The intention was that the public art program could be interpreted by the silence moments, and singular practices of daily life in the village.

Why was it important to project Revém Natura outside? How do you see your work in conversation with the environment?

The experience was conceived to be in any

public/open space. Then a grant by the Brazilian government and the reception of the community made it possible. This CI.NE (Natural Expanded Cinema) experience intends to arrange the conditions to the emergence of a self-consistent aggregate. The heterogenous elements (projectors, sunset, film, ambient sounds, prepared screens, etc) were invited to the compound. The flux between their differences generates this cine-haptic state. The artist Hélio Oiticica once said something that was really important to me. I'm not sure how to translate it, but it's something like "anthropology is to swallow the environment". Revém Natura could had be an experience in that the environment swallows cinema and vice versa.

Your work has screened all over the world! Where was your favorite place to screen your work?
The good and the bad thing in working with reproducible media is the amplified possibility to circulate the works. The already existent structures (cinemas, experimental distribution centers, festivals) with their singular potency to evocate publics in different contexts around the world is amazing. The hard and maybe dangerous part is the decontextualization and the lost of politization that derive from that. In a lot of screening and exhibitions I wasn't personally present. In some others I have been—especially with Revém Natura because of the performance aspect.

My favorite screening of Ravém Natura was in Teotihuacán, Mexico. The Revém's Natura work in progress was exhibited in a shaman's encounter! The meeting called Tawanitnisuyo articulated different ancestral healings, therapeutic practices, agroecological knowledge and the inclusion of my work let me think about how transdisciplinary practices situated artistic practice. Another

screening that I was really happy to form part - not in person - was Crossroads 2018 in SFMoMA. The contracultural environment, Bruce Baile's heritage, the LGBTQ district in which the museum exist, and the presence of a filmmaker-programmer (Steve Polta) connected my practice with this community .

Jonas Mekas left us this year. Can you talk about your other film *Viva Jonas* and what Mekas meant to you?
Jonas is an inspiration! His community-based actions and his films meant a lot to me. I discovered his work while living as an immigrant in Buenos Aires and his resistance while living in inhumane conditions and yet still practicing poetry shocked me in a good way. *Viva Jonas!* was a simple way to make a homage after his death. We've been in contact since 2013 because of our .txt texto de cinema poetry translation project. When learned about his death the necessity of a homage came immediately to our minds-bodies. *Viva Jonas!* was the first part of it but we also created a public program in Modern Art Museum Cinemateque in Rio de Janeiro and in CCBB - a Cultural Center in São Paulo- in which we've shown Jonas' work. We also made a kind of performance lecture - called Linguametragem- and learned to cook Lithuanian bread. His legacy stands like an ethical compass for me.

What's next for you?
In September of this year we are releasing Portuguese and Spanish translations of Jonas Mekas' poetry book *Dienorašciai*. I've also been collaborating on a 16mm work with Deborah S. Philps and Tobias S. that had its first exhibition as a performance in Belgium this year. *Verdevermelhar* (Green turns red) should be released as a film too.

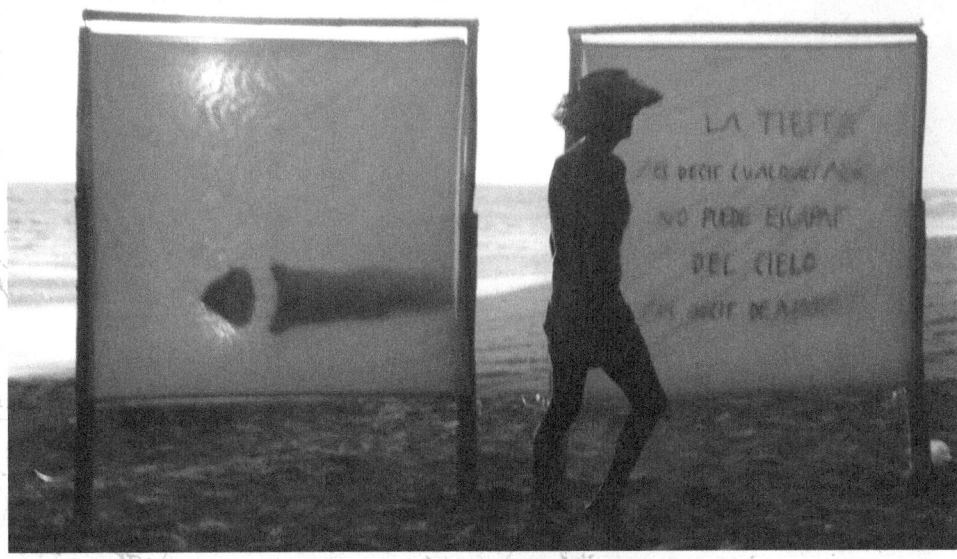

In Loving Memory

Barbara Hammer
Jonas Mekas
Carolee Schneemann
Phil Solomon
Agnes Varda
Brit Withey